DIVA Q'S
BARBECUE

DIVA Q'S BARBECUE

195 RECIPES FOR COOKING WITH FAMILY, FRIENDS & FIRE

Danielle Bennett

appetite
by RANDOM HOUSE

Appetite by Random House® and colophon are registered trademarks of Penguin Random House Canada LLC.

Library and Archives of Canada Cataloguing in Publication is available upon request.

ISBN: 978-0-14-752982-4
eBook ISBN: 978-0-14-752993-0

Photography by Ken Goodman
Photograph on pages iv-v by Robert Jacob Lerma
Photograph on page 276 by Doug Barlow
Apron on pages i and 3 © Alena Dudaeva | Dreamstime.com
Printed and bound in China

Published in Canada by Appetite by Random House®,
a division of Penguin Random House Canada Limited

www.penguinrandomhouse.ca

10 9 8 7 6 5 4 3 2

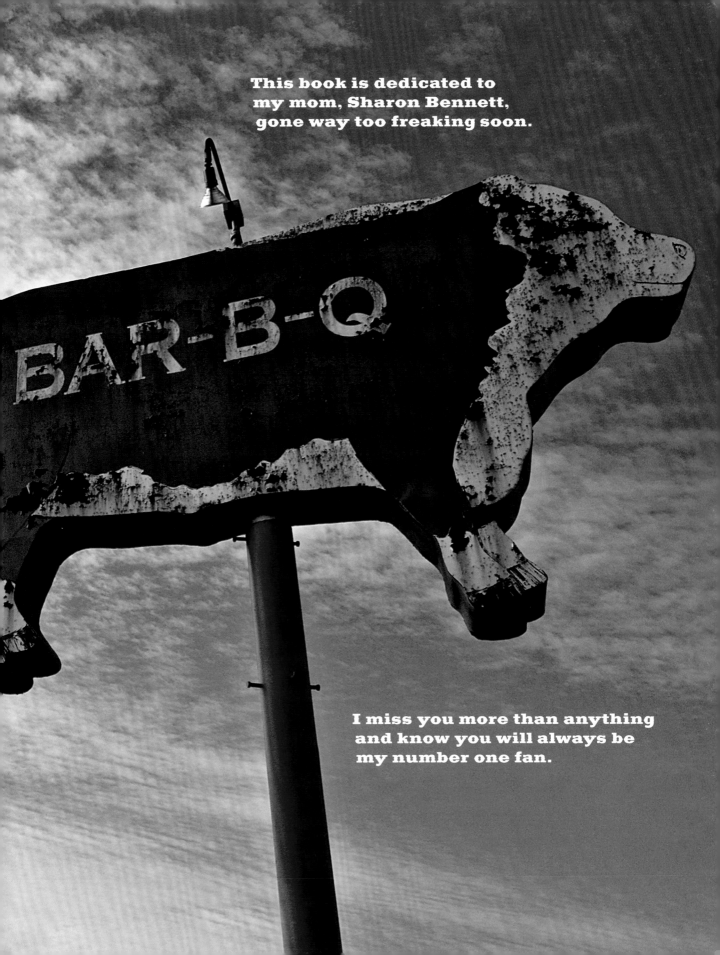

This book is dedicated to
my mom, Sharon Bennett,
gone way too freaking soon.

I miss you more than anything
and know you will always be
my number one fan.

"Danielle, aka Diva Q,
   is *the* most passionate person
   I know in barbecue."

—DAVE RAYMOND, aka SWEET BABY RAY

CONTENTS

FOREWORD

Yes, I know her real name is Danielle Bennett, but the first time I met her, Danielle introduced herself as Diva Q. So, for me, she will forever be Diva Q.

I met Diva Q one Sunday in July when she won her first barbecue trophy at the third annual Canadian Open Barbecue Championship in Barrie, ON. She took third place in the Best Ribs category, had a grin a mile wide and was screaming happy. Diva Q burst onto the barbecue scene that day.

She learned fire control, working with wood, and developed her love of smoking on her first Weber smoker—still her favorite, she says—and there was no looking back. She was on a roll then and is still moving and grooving the barbecue world today.

Diva Q and I have been friends and colleagues for ten years. A friend of mine who follows Diva Q's career says she's a female version of me. Scary to think she's my sister-from-another-mother kinda gal, but oh, what fun!

Diva Q's one awesome woman of the 'cue. She's anywhere there's barbecue: on the road, on TV, in the papers, in magazines, and on social media, including Twitter, Facebook, Pinterest and Instagram. You can subscribe to her YouTube channel (youtube.com/user/DivaQBBQ1) to watch how-to videos. I've learned a lot about social media from Diva Q.

You've got to be a little bit crazy to get involved with the world of competition barbecue, but Diva Q has the confidence, smarts and, above all, passion required to be a winner and end up with a résumé that includes:

- Jack Daniel's World Pork Champion, 2011
- World Bacon Champion, 2013
- Jack Daniel's I Know Jack . . . About Grillin' winner, 2013
- 15 grand championships
- 6 reserve grand championships
- More than 300 barbecue awards
- Hosting the hit TV show *BBQ Crawl*
- Appearances on TV shows *American Grilled*, *Today* and *BBQ Pitmasters*
- Inclusion in *Esquire* magazine's "BBQ Like a Man, According to Women"
- Sixteen perfect 180 scores from judges in barbecue competitions
- More US grand championships and awards than any other Canadian

Diva Q is a rock star of the barbecue world. Whether she's competing in a barbecue championship or cooking dinner for her family, Diva Q's heart goes into everything she does.

But Diva Q will tell you her family is the most important part of her life. Her kids love barbecue as much as their mom, and it's her family's pride and the love they deliver that keeps Diva Q laughing through the 30,000 to 40,000 miles she drives every year on the barbecue circuit.

When I asked Diva Q why she loves the crazy, smoky world of barbecue so much, she said, "Fire plus wood plus meat equals awesome, captivating, never-ending delicious fun. And the people make it special, too."

Competitive 'cuers are focused and intense. We keep our secret seasonings to ourselves and our eye on the prize. But once that chicken or brisket or those succulent Diva Q ribs have been delivered to the judges, we all come together as a close-knit family. We compare notes and cheer each other on. And in any gang of 'cuers, you'll find Diva Q right in the middle, laughing that great, infectious laugh of hers.

Diva Q is an absolutely fearless pitmaster, and she'll grill or smoke pretty much anything, just like I do. She even likes to bake on the grill. Her Buttery Cornbread with Forty Creek Honey Butter (page 235) is killer!

This book is a testament to straight-up good eating, Diva Q's way. She tells me her favorite recipe here is Cold-Smoked Cheddar-Pimento Cheese (page 48), so that's on my list, along with 180 Brisket (page 125). And I'll definitely be trying Get Your Jerk On! (page 152). I have a passion for jerk chicken and think mine's pretty darn good, but if Diva Q's got jerk, I know it's going to be amazing. Oh, and a dessert called Death by Diva (page 245) has to be nothing short of awesome.

This book will rock your taste buds. Inside is a collection of what a crazy guy like me calls the ultimate in comfort food. Let's face it, when our ancestors first cooked over a wood fire, they made barbecue the world's first comfort food. Diva Q is just helping us get back to our roots with this collection of her favorite recipes.

Jump into this book with the same passion Diva Q has. Learn from one of the best in the business, and make yourself some barbecue done right. Oh, it be a tasty barbecue world with Diva Q in it. Love you, Diva Q!

Cheers,

Ted Reader

Chef Ted Reader

FOR THE LOVE OF ALL THINGS BBQ

Whether noun, verb or adjective, barbecue is my passion. It's what I wake up thinking about each and every day. From the west coast to the east, I've traveled all over North America, visiting any place barbecue is served.

I have met some of the most amazing folks, all with an insatiable passion for barbecue. It doesn't matter to me whether they're cooking in a one-man shack on the side of the road or using the latest in barbecue technology. I want it all.

What is barbecue? I have no definitive answer, but believe it can be anything from a simple grilled steak to a beautiful slow-smoked brisket.

I love everything about barbecue: that first sizzle when meat hits the grill, then the gradual change from pink to mahogany as it cooks; the smell of wood smoke and the glow of hot coals on a perfect night.

I love everyone in the barbecue community and the passionate debates we have about the variations in regional barbecue recipes. And I love the thrill of barbecue competitions and the intensity of the chase.

Above all things, I love feeding people—especially my family and friends. These are the simple recipes I use again and again. Life's too short for bad barbecue.

Diva Q

DIVA Q'S
HOUSE RULES

- Get your grill on by preparing all your ingredients before you start cooking.

- A clean grill is a good grill, so clean it well before cooking.

- Preheat properly. Make sure you heat the grill to the correct temperature.

- Stop the sticky! Oil your grill before the food goes on.

- Keep the bad bugs away. Have two sets of tongs and plates, one for the raw meat and one for the cooked.

- Make sure your fire extinguisher is kitchen-rated, and know where it is at all times. Never throw water on a grease fire; use your fire extinguisher.

- If you're looking, you're not cooking: keep that lid closed.

- Don't squish down your burgers—you'll let the yummy out.

- Apply sauce only during the last few minutes of cooking.

- Pink can be okay. Use a digital thermometer to check the internal temperature of your food.

- Have patience. It's done when it's done.

- Give it a rest already. Let your cooked meat rest before slicing into it.

- Remember to have fun. Grilling outdoors can be a great escape.

BARBECUE BASICS

Check out the What You Need to Get Your Grill On section at the back of the book for my favorite grills and gear, then nail the tips in this chapter and you're well on your way to good barbecue.

BARBECUE OR GRILL: WHAT'S THE DIFF?

Many people use these terms interchangeably, but here's the scoop:

Traditionally, barbecue is food cooked low and slow over indirect heat (see below), with temperatures ranging from 225°F to 275°F.

Grilling cooks the food over higher direct heat (see below).

KNOW YOUR FIRE

Whether you're barbecuing or grilling, lesson number one is understanding your fire. To be a good barbecuer, you need to learn how to use charcoal and wood properly and to maintain and adjust temperatures. Here are some of the fire management basics you need to know before you get your 'cue on!

INDIRECT HEAT Knowing how to create an indirect fire zone is essential.

Pellet grills (see page 260) have this feature built into their design and run indirect heat through the entire cooking process.

Charcoal, wood and gas grills (see page 260) all require you to move the charcoal or adjust the heat source to provide an area for indirect cooking. In a charcoal grill, you can bank all the coals to one side, or you can place an aluminum pan in the middle and bank charcoal on either side of the pan. The heat is not even, but you have created a zone that has no direct flames.

For charcoal kettle grills, create a ring of fire by banking all the coals around the outer edge of the kettle. The center of the grate will then be your indirect cooking area.

On a gas grill, turn off all the burners but one. Or if you're using a large multiple-burner gas grill, turn the center burners off, leaving the left and right burners on.

DIRECT HEAT Grilling over direct heat is the most basic way to cook. You start a fire and food is cooked directly above it. Anything you want to grill quickly should be done over direct heat.

Any proteins 2 inches or less in thickness can be cooked by this method. Traditional grilled items like steaks, burgers, sliced veggies and fish all fall into this category. More than 2 inches and you need a combination of direct and indirect cooking.

Your grill's lid can be up or down depending on how fast you want to cook: leave the lid up and the heat escapes; close the lid and the food is surrounded by the trapped heat.

If grilling over charcoal, you need an even layer of charcoal. Peaks and valleys in the layering of your charcoal will create swings in the grate-level temperature. Keeping the coals an even thickness all the way across the bottom of your charcoal grill ensures temperature swings will be minimal.

PLANKING ▶ Planking is the use of soaked wooden planks on which to cook food over a fire source. Planks must be from untreated wood and can range in size from a small piece for a single portion of salmon to a large plank for cooking a whole fish or other large pieces of protein.

MULTIPLE-LAYER FIRES When you are grilling many different items at once on your grill, you may want some areas to be hotter than others.

On a **charcoal grill**, arrange a single layer of charcoal for lower-heat cooking on one side of the grill and multiple layers of charcoal for hotter cooking on the other side. The closer the coals are to the grate, the hotter the fire will be.

On a **gas grill**, simply adjust the temperature of the burners to create hotter and cooler areas for cooking.

TEMPERATURE GUIDELINES How hot is hot? Here's a guide to the temperatures I use in my recipes:

HIGH HEAT: 450°F-PLUS Use this temperature to cook thin cuts of meat, sear steaks and char items. You should never walk more than a foot or two away from the grill when using this temperature range. Most times the lid will be open.

MEDIUM-HIGH HEAT: 375°F TO 450°F The majority of grilling happens in this temperature zone. Hot enough to make great-looking grill marks yet still give you time to move things around before they burn, it's good for burgers, sliced vegetables and chops.

MEDIUM HEAT: 300°F TO 375°F This temperature range cuts right down the middle and is great if you need a bit more time to move items around the grill. You can still get the perfect crust on your meat—it will just take a little bit longer.

LOW TO MEDIUM-LOW HEAT: 200°F TO 300°F Perfect for indirect cooking of big pieces of meat, this temperature range is where traditional low and slow barbecuing occurs.

GRILLING GUIDELINES

The grilling times listed in the guidelines below are meant as a very general reference guide only, and not as a hard and fast rule book. Every item included can take a little more or a little less time than is listed here as there are so many factors that can impact the time it takes to cook something: Size in particular matters in all things grilling, for example large scallops will take much longer than their smaller counterparts. Instead of judging doneness by time I use a digital thermometer (see page 261) to test the internal temperature of the meat. This is far and away *the most accurate way* to ensure that you get perfect grill results every time. See the minimum internal temperatures column of the chart to know what you're looking for with every different cut of meat.

For more information on high, medium and low heat ranges see page 5.

FOOD	DONENESS (IF APPLICABLE)	METHOD (DIRECT OR INDIRECT)	HEAT	TIME	MINIMUM INTERNAL TEMPERATURE
BEEF					
Steak (½ inch thick)	Extra-rare or blue (*bleu*)	D	High	2 to 4 min	100°F
	Rare	D	High	3 to 6 min	120°F
	Medium-rare	D	High	5 to 8 min	135°F
	Medium	D	High	6 to 9 min	145°F
	Medium-well	D	High	7 to 10 min	155°F
	Well done	D	High	9 to 12 min	160°F
Roast	Rare	I	Low	18 to 22 min per lb	120°F
	Medium	I	Low	22 to 28 min per lb	145°F
	Well done	I	Low	28 to 32 min per lb	160°F
Brisket		I	Low	10 to 14 hr	180°F to 205°F
Ground	Well done	D	Medium	10 to 15 min	160°F
PORK					
Chops (½ inch thick)	Medium	D	High	8 to 12 min	140°F
	Well done	D	High	15 to 20 min	155°F to 160°F
Roast	Medium	I	Medium	18 to 22 min per lb	140°F
	Well done	I	Medium	25 to 35 min per lb	155°F to 160°F
Ribs		I	Low	4 to 5 hr	180°F to 205°F
Shoulder		I	Low	8 to 10 hr	180°F to 205°F
Ham, uncooked (smoked)		I	Medium	18 to 22 min per lb	160°F
Ham, precooked (reheated)		I	Medium	18 to 22 min per lb	140°F
Ground	Well done	D	Medium	10 to 15 min	160°F
Sausage, uncooked (raw)	Well done	D	Medium	18 to 22 min	160°F
Sausage, precooked (reheated)	Well done	D	Medium	10 to 15 min	140°F

FOOD	DONENESS (IF APPLICABLE)	METHOD (DIRECT OR INDIRECT)	HEAT	TIME	MINIMUM INTERNAL TEMPERATURE
LAMB					
Chops (½ inch thick)	Rare	D	High	3 to 5 min	115°F
	Medium-rare	D	High	4 to 7 min	125°F
	Medium	D	High	5 to 8 min	135°F
	Medium-well	D	High	6 to 9 min	150°F
	Well done	D	High	8 to 12 min	160°F
Ground	Well done	D	Medium	10 to 15 min	160°F
POULTRY					
Chicken broiler/fryer (3 to 4 lb)		I	Low	75 to 90 min	165°F (breast), 175°F (thigh)
Chicken, halved		I	Low	40 to 60 min	165°F (breast), 175°F (thigh)
Chicken breasts		I	Medium	20 to 30 min	165°F
Chicken thighs		I	Medium	20 to 30 min	175°F
Chicken wings		I	High	20 to 30 min	175°F
Turkey, whole		I	Low	18 to 22 min per lb	165°F (breast), 175°F (thigh)
Ground		I	Medium	10 to 15 min	165°F
FISH AND SHELLFISH					
Steaks (1 inch thick)		I	Medium	10 to 15 min	125°F (tuna, swordfish and marlin)
Fillets (6 to 8 oz)		I	Medium	8 to 12 min	145°F (cod, halibut, red snapper, tilapia, salmon and sea bass)
Crab cakes		D	Medium	8 to 10 min	155°F
Lobster		D	Medium	8 to 10 min	145°F
Scallops		D	Medium	8 to 10 min	120°F
Shrimp (large or jumbo)		I	Medium	8 to 12 min	120°F
VEGETABLES					
Potatoes, whole		I	Low	50 to 60 min	n/a
Onions, whole		I	Low	40 to 50 min	n/a
Peppers, halved		D	High	15 to 20 min	n/a
Tomatoes, halved		D	Medium	20 to 30 min	n/a
Asparagus, whole		D	High	10 to 15 min	n/a
Corn, whole		D	Medium	35 to 45 min	n/a
Mushrooms, halved		D	Medium	15 to 20 min	n/a

* If in doubt about the safe internal temperature of food, consult the guidelines on your federal health website.

KNOW YOUR GRILL

HOT SPOTS Whether you're using a pellet grill, charcoal grill or gas grill, every grill is different and has hot spots where the food will cook more quickly or even scorch.

To test your grill for hot spots, buy several cans of refrigerator biscuits. (It's a lot more economical to spend a few dollars on biscuits than to wreck an expensive piece of meat.) Fire up your grill and, while it's heating, open the cans and separate the biscuits. Arrange the biscuits on your grill to cover the grate completely. As the biscuits start to brown, you'll soon be able to tell exactly where the hot spots are.

AIR FLOW CONTROL Charcoal needs oxygen, so when cooking on a charcoal grill, you need to know how to work the air vents. Does your grill have one, two or even three vents? To figure out how the oxygen travels through those vents and into your cooking chamber, use the biscuit method above.

Light the grill and open one vent. Arrange the biscuits on the cooking grate to cover it completely. Continue opening and closing each vent until you've opened them all. Watch how the biscuits brown to learn how each vent affects the heat of your grill.

BABY, LIGHT MY FIRE

Every grill comes with an owner's manual, so take the time to read it from cover to cover so you know how to light your grill safely. In all cases, the lighting instructions in the manual should take precedence over any of mine. Seriously. They print those things for a reason.

CHARCOAL GRILLS Lighting charcoal takes patience, but a chimney starter (see page 262) speeds things up. Use either all-natural lump charcoal or competition briquettes. Do not use lighter fluid, which can leave a bad aftertaste on food and has no redeeming value other than speed.

Set the chimney starter on a patio stone or other non-flammable surface. Lay a couple of pieces of paper towel sprayed with cooking oil in the bottom of the chimney. Fill the chimney with charcoal. Light the paper towel with a barbecue lighter. When the charcoal is glowing red and ashed over, carefully pour it into the cooking chamber.

Instead of paper towel, you can use natural or waxed fire starter cubes. Fill the chimney with charcoal. Place the fire starter cubes under the chimney and set the chimney on a nonflammable surface. Light the cubes with a barbecue lighter. Wait until the charcoal is glowing and ashed over before pouring it into the cooking chamber.

For longer cooks, you may want to line your cooking chamber with a layer of unlit charcoal before adding the glowing charcoal to it. Take the time to arrange the unlit charcoal so there's very little space between the pieces. Tighter-packed piles of charcoal last longer. The more open space between the pieces of charcoal, the cooler the fire and the faster it will go out.

PELLET GRILLS Fill the hopper with *food-safe* pellets. Open the lid. Turn the switch or dial to the On position and set the temperature to Smoke. Wait for two to three minutes until you see smoke, which indicates the igniter in the fire pot has lit the pellets. Close the lid and adjust the controls to the desired temperature.

CERAMIC BARBECUES See the instructions for lighting a charcoal grill (above).

GAS GRILLS To light a natural gas or propane grill, follow the manufacturer's instructions.

HOW TO GET GREAT CHAR MARKS

You know them and you love them—those beautiful grilling marks that make your mouth water and make you want to dig in right away! Here is how you get them.

GET YOUR SMOKE ON

It's easy to add great smoke flavor to anything you grill. To team the right wood with the right meat, check out wood and meat pairing recommendations on page 10. When I use wood chunks or chips, I don't usually soak them in water before adding them to the grill. But if you want to add a little more humidity to your grill, feel free to soak wood chips or chunks in water for at least thirty minutes, then drain them before using.

PELLET GRILLS are one of the simplest grills to use for smoking. For large cuts of meat, simply set the dial to its lowest temperature (about 180°F) and let the wood pellets do all the work. To ramp up the smoke flavor, you can add a smoking tube filled with additional burning pellets or a tray of wood dust to the grill. Check your manufacturer's instructions for more information.

GAS GRILLS are easy to adapt for smoking. Prepare your grill for indirect cooking (see page 4). Fill a smoker box (see page 262) with wood chips and place it on the hot side of the grill. Wait until the wood chips start to smoke before putting your food on the cool side of the grill. Depending on the size of the pieces of food and the length of time you're smoking them, you may need to replenish the wood chips every thirty minutes or so to maintain the smoke flavor.

CHARCOAL GRILLS should be prepared for indirect cooking (see page 4). Add wood chunks or chips directly to the charcoal. Wait until the wood chunks or chips start to smoke before putting your food on the cool side of the grill. Depending on the size of the pieces of food and the length of time you're smoking them, you may need to replenish the wood chunks or chips every thirty minutes or so to maintain the smoke flavor.

HOW TO GET GREAT CHAR MARKS

WOOD AND MEAT PAIRING RECOMMENDATIONS

Wood and wood smoke are great additional ingredients to add to any meal. Pairing the right wood with the right food is an important step for barbecue happiness. Take a look at some of my favorite pairings below.

WOOD	INTENSITY	FLAVOR	BEEF	PORK	HAM	LAMB	POULTRY	WILD GAME	FISH (EXCLUDING SALMON)	SALMON	CHEESE
Alder	Mild	Light and sweet		X			X		X	X	
Almond	Mild	Nutty and sweet	X	X			X				
Apple	Strong	Light and fruity		X	X		X				
Apricot	Mild	Sweet		X	X		X		X		
Cherry	Mild	Mild and fruity	X	X			X		X	X	
Grapevine	Medium	Rich and fruity	X			X	X	X			
Hickory	Strong	Classic smoke flavor	X	X	X		X	X			
Lilac	Mild	Hint of floral				X			X		
Maple	Mild	Mellow and sweet		X	X		X				X
Mesquite	Strong	Sweet and spicy	X	X			X	X	X		
Mulberry	Mild	Sweet and tangy	X		X		X				
Oak	Mild	Mild and nutty	X	X		X	X		X		
Orange	Mild	Tangy citrus		X			X		X		X
Peach	Mild	Sweet and woodsy	X	X			X		X		
Pear	Mild	Sweet and woodsy		X			X				
Pecan	Mild	Milder than hickory	X	X			X		X		X
Plum	Mild	Sweet and woodsy		X			X		X		
Walnut	Very strong	Heavy smoke	X					X			

SOURCES: fruitawoodchunks.com; bbq-brethren.com; smoked-meat.com

BUTCHERS ROCK!

My number one tip for finding the best meat for your grill is to get to know your butcher. Period. Find one and form a relationship with him or her. Visit the store often.

My go-to butcher for most meats is Brian Witteveen of Strodes BBQ and Deli in Brantford, ON (strodes.ca). Brian comes from a long line of butchers, and we have been friends for more than ten years. He gives me the best advice about what cuts of meat to buy and recommends new cuts when they come along. I love my butcher.

Source the highest-quality meat your budget allows. Quality always trumps quantity, and it's more rewarding to spend more money on smaller yet higher-quality, better-marbled pieces of meat. The better the meat, the better the barbecue.

As much as possible, know where your meat comes from. I buy most of my pork directly from pork farmer Paul Hill of Willowgrove Hill, near Stratford, ON (willowgrovehill.com). I have visited Paul's farm and seen how well he takes care of his pigs.

CHILLIN' AND GRILLIN'

Snow *never* prevents me from getting my grill on. I barbecue and grill year-round. Here's what I've learned:

- Shovel out a safe path to your grill before you start. There's nothing worse than dropping that freshly barbecued dinner in the snow!
- Clean all the snow from around your grill and off the top before you start.

- Wind is your biggest enemy in the winter, so try to locate your grill in a sheltered spot.
- Before using a gas grill in the winter, check the hoses for any cracks.
- Don't wear a dangling scarf or a loose-fitting winter coat.
- Food takes longer to cook in the winter, and your grill will take longer to warm up. Give yourself extra time for dinner.
- Select tried-and-true, easy recipes for winter grilling. This is not the time to be trying out a new ten-course meal.
- Use recipes that call for just a single flip. Less fiddling with the food makes for happier winter grilling.
- Get to know how to cook on your grill using indirect heat. Larger cuts of meat that require less attention work well in the winter.
- If you're looking, you're not cooking. Keep the lid closed as much as you can—the grill will lose heat faster in the winter.
- If you're cooking with charcoal, you will go through more when cooking in the winter. Use good-quality lump charcoal with a low moisture level.
- It gets dark a lot earlier in the winter, so invest in a grill light, outdoor patio lantern or other light source.
- Frozen fat is harder to clean, so wipe up your drips immediately.
- A snow pile makes a great beer holder.

CHECK OUT THE COMPETITION

Most barbecue competitions let the public come and watch, and we competitors love that they do. If you plan to visit a competition near you, here are a few tips on competitive-barbecue etiquette:

- Barbecue teams pay not only for their meat and supplies, but also a fee to take part in the competition. Most teams take competing very seriously.
- If you see someone walking with a turn-in box (usually a 9- × 9-inch Styrofoam container) containing competition barbecue, please move out of the way.
- If you see someone walking with a tray of food items, please move out of the way.
- Do not under any circumstances ever take any food from tables within a competition site without asking. Most competitions do not allow public sampling. Please visit the vendors at the site to purchase food and support the event.
- Be respectful of the competition site. Do not cut through a team's site to get to another section of the competition area. That's like walking through someone's house.
- Mind your manners and your children. Children and their parents should be aware that there are hot grills and sharp knives at every site. Do not let your children run around team sites. Do not let your drunk friends run around team sites either.
- Do not touch another person's grills *ever*, or not without asking first.
- The clock rules everything during a competition. Teams need to turn in items on a specific schedule. During those turn-in times, competitors may not want to stop and talk. It's nothing personal. Turn-in times vary, but usually run from 11:30 am to 2:00 pm.
- Please ask before taking photos of teams preparing their entries. Some teams would rather not have pictures of their items in the public domain.
- Ask questions of teams when they're not busy. We love to talk about all things barbecue.
- Some events have adult beverage tents. Please enjoy them responsibly.
- There are quiet hours at every barbecue contest. Please respect them.
- Please come out to the awards ceremony and cheer for all the teams. The more the merrier.
- Visit team websites like mine (divaq.ca) or that of the Kansas City Barbeque Society (kcbs.us) for more information about competition barbecue.

Cold-Smoked Cheese (page 18)

SIX RECIPES YOU NEED TO KNOW

The following recipes are my go-to barbecue basics. Four of them are must-try recipes I refer to often in the book. As well, you'll find my definitive, killer recipes for burgers and steak.

Basic Brine

MAKES: about 4 cups (enough for 4 to 6 chicken breasts or pork chops) • **PREP:** 5 minutes

Brining chicken and pork before barbecuing keeps the meat nice and juicy on the grill.

4 cups water
¼ cup kosher salt
2 tbsp packed brown sugar
1 tsp whole black peppercorns
1 tsp whole allspice berries

1. In a medium plastic container, whisk together all the ingredients until the salt and sugar dissolve. **2.** Submerge raw meat in the brine and let soak, allowing 1 hour per pound of meat. **3.** Remove the meat from the brine and pat dry before cooking.

Q SAVVY

For kosher salt I always use good-quality Morton Salt, as sodium levels vary greatly from brand to brand.

• •

Add sprigs of fresh herbs, like rosemary and thyme, to the brine for extra flavor.

Smoked Garlic

MAKES: 20 bulbs • **PREP:** 10 minutes • **COOK:** 2 to 4 hours

I am a big believer in using a grill to its full capacity when I light it up. It makes no sense to smoke just one garlic bulb at a time, so I like to make a big batch. Smoked garlic freezes really well and is super handy. Add it to soups, stocks or dips (try making an aioli with it), or spread it on toast points or crusty bread and drizzle with good-quality olive oil.

Hickory wood chips
20 bulbs garlic
1 cup extra virgin olive oil
¼ cup kosher salt
¼ cup finely ground black pepper

1. Prepare your smoker or grill for indirect cooking, and preheat it to 375°F to 450°F. Add a handful of hickory chips, following the instructions on page 9 for your type of smoker or grill. **2.** Using a sharp knife, cut a ¼-inch slice from the top of each garlic bulb, making sure the individual cloves of garlic are exposed. **3.** Place the bulbs in a disposable aluminum pan. Drizzle with olive oil and sprinkle with salt and pepper. **4.** When the chips are smoking, place the pan of garlic bulbs on the cool side of the grill. Smoke the garlic for 1 hour, then cover the pan with foil. **5.** Continue smoking until the cloves are softened, caramelized and browned, 1 to 3 hours. Replenish the hickory chips by adding another handful every 30 minutes while the garlic smokes. **6.** Remove the pan from the grill and let the garlic bulbs cool completely. Wrap the bulbs individually and freeze for up to 3 months.

Q SAVVY

You can add extra flavor to your smoked garlic by substituting blended salts like chipotle or porcini for the kosher salt in this recipe.

Flavored Butters

MAKES: about ½ cup • **PREP:** 10 minutes • **CHILL:** at least 2 hours

Flavored butters are easy to whip up and perfect for topping grilled meats, seafood and vegetables, especially corn.

½ cup unsalted butter, softened

Cilantro-Lime Butter

¼ cup chopped fresh cilantro
1 lime, zested and juiced
½ tsp kosher salt
½ tsp finely ground black pepper

Garlic-Chive Butter

6 cloves Smoked Garlic (page 15), smashed
2 tbsp finely chopped fresh chives
½ tsp kosher salt
½ tsp finely ground black pepper

Blue Cheese Butter

2 tbsp crumbled blue cheese
½ tsp kosher salt
½ tsp finely ground black pepper

Smoked Paprika–Bacon Butter

2 tbsp minced cooked bacon
1 tbsp sweet smoked paprika
½ tsp kosher salt
½ tsp finely ground black pepper

1. Whip the softened butter with the flavorings of your choice.
2. Spoon the butter onto a sheet of plastic wrap, then use the plastic wrap to form the butter into a log shape. Wrap the butter tightly in the plastic wrap. Chill for at least 2 hours until firm.
3. Unwrap the butter and cut into slices to serve.

Q SAVVY

Flavored butters freeze well and are great to have on hand to dress up last-minute grilled steak dinners.

Cold-Smoked Cheese Photo on page 12

MAKES: 1 lb • **PREP:** 5 minutes • **COOK:** 1½ to 2 hours

Run-of-the-mill cheese can be turned into something unique with the addition of a little smoke. Any low-moisture, firm cheese can be smoked. My favorites are sharp or marbled cheddar, friulano, mozzarella, low-moisture provolone or pepper Jack. You can smoke several types of cheese at once. Just make sure the cheese is cut into one-pound blocks and is as far away from the heat source as possible. Use the smoked cheese in recipes or serve with smoked sausage, crackers and pickles.

1 lb cheese (see note above)
Wood chips (see sidebar)

1. Prepare your smoker or grill for indirect cooking and preheat it to 90°F (the temperature needs to be very low). If using a charcoal grill, use only a couple of pieces of charcoal. **2.** Add a handful of wood chips, following the instructions on page 9 for your type of smoker or grill. **3.** When the chips start to smoke, place the cheese as far away from the heat source as possible. Smoke for 1½ to 2 hours. Replenish the wood chips by adding another handful every 30 minutes while the cheese smokes.

Q SAVVY

Every cheese takes on the smoke differently, so experiment by pairing different cheeses with different woods. I like cheddar and hickory, mozzarella and maple, and provolone and oak. As you store the smoked cheese, its flavor will become more pronounced.

Basic Big Burgers

MAKES: 6 burgers • **PREP:** 15 minutes • **COOK:** 10 to 13 minutes

I like to make a depression in the center of each burger as I form it. As the burger cooks, the center will puff up and the burger will cook more evenly. These are big burgers, so make sure your buns measure up.

3 lb ground beef (80% lean, 20% fat)
Kosher salt and finely ground black
    pepper to taste
Canola oil
6 hamburger buns

1. Prepare your grill for direct cooking and preheat it to medium-high heat (375°F to 450°F). **2.** Divide the meat into six even-size portions and form into burgers. Press the center of each burger down to create a depression. Season burgers generously on both sides with salt and pepper. **3.** Oil the grill grate with canola oil. Grill the burgers on one side until lightly crusted over, 4 to 5 minutes. Flip the burgers and grill the opposite side until the internal temperature reaches 160°F, 6 to 8 minutes.

Q SAVVY

Pimp your basic burgers with these add-ins:

Greek Burgers
Add 1 tbsp dried Greek oregano and 1 tbsp minced garlic to the ground beef. Top the burgers with tzatziki, sliced red onion and pitted black olives.

Mexican Burgers
Add 1 tbsp chili powder, 2 tsp onion powder, 2 tsp minced garlic and 1 tsp ground cumin to the ground beef. Top the burgers with lettuce, pepper Jack and your favorite salsa.

Reverse-Seared Steaks

MAKES: 4 servings • **PREP:** 5 minutes • **COOK:** 25 to 30 minutes

Reverse searing—grilling over low, indirect heat before a final sear—gives your steaks a terrific crust and the most evenly cooked and juiciest meat possible. You can use this method for all types of steak.

4 steaks (1½ inches thick)
2 tbsp canola oil
Montreal Steak Spice (page 26)

1. Prepare your grill for indirect cooking and preheat it to 225°F. **2.** Lightly oil each steak on both sides with canola oil and season generously with Montreal Steak Spice. **3.** Place the steaks on the cool side of the grill. Grill, flipping once, until their internal temperature reaches 115°F, 20 to 25 minutes. **4.** Remove the steaks from the grill and tent lightly with foil. Prepare the grill for direct cooking and increase the temperature to 500°F. **5.** Grill the steaks over direct heat, flipping every 2 minutes, until the desired internal temperature has been reached (see sidebar). **6.** Remove the steaks from the grill. Tent the steaks with foil and let rest for 5 minutes before slicing or serving.

Q SAVVY

Make your digital meat thermometer your friend and get perfect steaks every time. Insert the thermometer horizontally through the side of the steak to check for doneness.

- *Rare: 120°F*
- *Medium-rare: 130°F*
- *Medium: 145°F*
- *Medium-well: 155°F*
- *Well done: 160°F*

RUBS, SAUCES, SLATHERS
& SPICES

Team great meat with a tasty rub, sauce, slather or spice and you have a winning combination. From sweet to savory—and everything in between—these seasonings will perk up your taste buds.

Diva Q Pork and Chicken Rub

MAKES: about 2 cups • **PREP:** 10 minutes

This is my go-to rub for so many things. It's not too sweet, not too savory and perfect for all things pork and chicken. It makes a big batch and stores well in a mason jar. For most oomph, use the freshest spices possible.

1 cup packed light brown sugar

¼ cup sweet smoked paprika

3 tbsp good-quality kosher salt

2 tbsp coarsely ground Malabar black pepper (see sidebar)

2 tbsp chili powder

2 tbsp granulated onion (see page 25)

2 tbsp granulated garlic (see page 25)

2 tsp piri piri or chipotle powder

1 tsp ground cumin

1 tsp ground coriander

1 tsp ground thyme

1. Mix together all the ingredients in a medium bowl. Store in an airtight container. **2.** Rub on pork or chicken before grilling.

Q SAVVY

Stir Diva Q Pork and Chicken Rub into cream cheese or sour cream for a fantastic topping for baked potatoes.

Malabar black pepper comes from southwest India, where the best black pepper is grown. If you can't find it, substitute regular black pepper.

Memphis Rib Rub

MAKES: about ¹/₃ cup (enough for 1 rack of ribs) • **PREP:** 10 minutes

Memphis, TN, is home to a whole lot of great barbecue. My fave places to try it are Cozy Corner Bar-B-Q, Germantown Commissary and The Bar-B-Q Shop. Each serves fabulous rubbed ribs, but none of the restaurants would share its secret. No matter—I came up with my own rub. Sometimes experimenting until you get it right is one of the best things about barbecue. This rub is perfect for making dry ribs without any sauce.

4 tsp sweet smoked paprika

2 tsp kosher salt

2 tsp onion powder

2 tsp finely ground black pepper

2 tsp granulated brown sugar

1 tsp chili powder

1 tsp dried thyme leaves

1 tsp dried oregano leaves

1 tsp mild mustard powder

¼ tsp ground allspice

1. Mix together all the ingredients in a small bowl. Store in an airtight container. **2.** Rub on ribs before grilling.

Q SAVVY

Prefer it spicy? Just add 2 tsp chipotle or habanero powder.

Cajun Rub

MAKES: about ³/₄ cup (enough for 1 rack of ribs or 1 chicken) • **PREP:** 10 minutes

My dear friends at Mister Jug Shrimp in Lafitte, LA, took me out on their shrimp trawler one day. It was a spectacular adventure, and at the end of it we indulged in a delicious Cajun dish made from beautiful freshly caught Louisiana shrimp. Mister Jug Shrimp's rub is a closely guarded secret. All I know is, the moment I tasted it, I knew I had to do my best to recreate it. This Cajun Rub makes anything taste good—probably even cardboard. Or add it to melted butter and drizzle it over your favorite grilled catch of the day.

2 tbsp sweet smoked paprika

2 tsp kosher salt

2 tsp granulated onion (see sidebar)

2 tsp granulated garlic (see sidebar)

2 tsp cayenne

1½ tsp finely ground white pepper

1 tsp ground thyme

1 tsp dried oregano leaves

½ tsp finely ground black pepper

1. Mix together all the ingredients in a small bowl. Store in an airtight container. **2.** Rub on seafood, poultry or pork before grilling.

Q SAVVY

You'll notice some of my recipes call for granulated onion (or garlic), others for onion (or garlic) powder. They're very different, so check the jar labels carefully. The granulated version creates more of a crust on meats, while the powdered is more readily absorbed.

Kansas City Rub

MAKES: about 1¹/₃ cups • **PREP:** 10 minutes

There's so much to love about Kansas City, MO. It's a mecca of barbecue, and I'm blessed to have so many great friends there, all of whom make incredible 'cue (although maybe I'm a little biased). Kansas City offers a wide variety of barbecue styles, sauces and rubs. I have always been a fan of the sweet-spicy balance of this one.

½ cup granulated brown sugar, such as Domino Brownulated (see sidebar)

¼ cup granulated sugar

¼ cup sweet smoked paprika

1 tbsp medium-grind black pepper

1 tbsp kosher salt

1 tbsp chili powder

1 tbsp garlic powder

1 tbsp onion powder

1 tsp cayenne

1. Mix together all the ingredients in a small bowl. Store in an airtight container. **2.** Rub on seafood, poultry or pork before grilling.

Q SAVVY

Granulated brown sugar is a pourable brown sugar that doesn't lump or harden. If you can't find it, spread out regular brown sugar on a baking sheet and let it air-dry overnight. Sift the sugar, then measure and add to the rub.

Montreal Steak Spice

MAKES: about 1 cup • **PREP:** 10 minutes

Canada has a lot of great exports and, like hockey and maple syrup, our Montreal steak spice is legendary. Sure, you can buy it, but it tastes way better if you make it yourself. I have given this rub as a gift to my family and friends and always have a batch on hand. It's like salt and pepper in our house, and is a handy all-round rub. Use it generously on steaks, roasts and thick-cut pork chops.

3 tbsp kosher salt

3 tbsp coarsely ground black pepper (butcher grind)

2 tbsp sweet smoked paprika

2 tbsp granulated onion (see page 25)

2 tbsp granulated garlic (see page 25)

1 tbsp dill seed

1 tbsp ground coriander

1 tbsp dehydrated sweet red pepper flakes

1 tbsp mustard powder

1. Mix together all the ingredients in a small bowl. Leave as is for a coarser mixture or, if you prefer, transfer to a spice grinder and grind until finely ground, 10 to 15 seconds. Store in an airtight container. **2.** Rub on beef or pork before grilling.

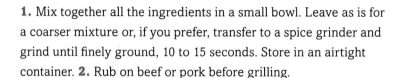

Q SAVVY

For a spicier seasoning, swap out the sweet red pepper flakes for hot red pepper flakes and add 1 tbsp chipotle powder or cayenne.

Canadian Rub

MAKES: about ½ cup • **PREP:** 10 minutes

O Canada! The true north, strong and free. Ah, maple! You gotta love it. This Canuck just had to come up with a rub using that quintessential Canadian ingredient. Granulated maple sugar adds richer flavor to rubs than regular granulated sugar and a beautiful deep color to the food it's rubbed on.

¼ cup granulated maple sugar

2 tsp chili powder

2 tsp garlic powder

2 tsp onion powder

2 tsp kosher salt

1 tsp sweet smoked paprika

1 tsp celery seed

½ tsp cinnamon

½ tsp chipotle powder

½ tsp ground cumin

1. Mix together all the ingredients in a small bowl. Store in an airtight container. **2.** Rub on seafood, poultry or pork before grilling.

Q SAVVY

Want to ramp up the maple and give your meats a rich, dark hue? Slather them with maple syrup prior to applying the rub. Just be careful to use indirect heat, as the sugars will caramelize and may burn.

Greek Rub

MAKES: about ³/₄ cup • **PREP:** 10 minutes

For a flavorful marinade or baste for pork, poultry or seafood, mix a batch of this rub with ½ cup canola oil and the finely grated zest and squeezed juice of 2 large lemons.

2 tbsp dried Greek oregano leaves

2 tbsp kosher salt

2 tbsp dried basil

1 tbsp dried dill weed

1 tbsp garlic powder

2 tsp lemon pepper

2 tsp finely ground black pepper

2 tsp dried parsley leaves

1 tsp dried marjoram leaves

½ tsp ground thyme

1. Mix together all ingredients in a small bowl. Store in an airtight container. **2.** Rub on pork, poultry and seafood.

Spicy Thai Rub

MAKES: about ¹/₂ cup • **PREP** 10 minutes

I am a bit of a wuss about the whole spicy food thing. My friend Sieng (Sam) Duong, who is originally from Cambodia, laughs at my inability to handle heat. We've known Sam and his beautiful wife, Anna, since their kids, Michael and Angela, were at junior kindergarten with ours. When I was trying to come up with this rub, I asked Sam to try it. I knew I had a winner when he said he loved it. Full approval from Sam is a home run for me. Just a warning: this is seriously hot.

2 tbsp granulated onion (see page 25)

2 tbsp granulated garlic (see page 25)

2 tbsp packed light brown sugar

1 tbsp hot red pepper flakes, ground

1 tbsp ground turmeric

½ tbsp ground ginger

1 tsp powdered dried lemon peel

1 tsp ground coriander

1 tsp dried mint leaves

1. Mix together all the ingredients in a small bowl. Store in an airtight container. **2.** Rub on beef, pork, poultry and seafood or sprinkle on vegetables before grilling.

Q SAVVY

For Fresh Mint Thai Slather, finely chop the leaves from 1 small bunch of fresh mint and add to the rub along with ¾ cup canola oil and the zest and juice of 3 limes. Apply to meats prior to indirect grilling.

Espresso Rub

MAKES: about ¾ cup • **PREP:** 10 minutes

I am a coffee addict and drink, on average, about eight cups a day. There, I've admitted it. But instant espresso powder is also my secret ingredient in rubs, bringing out the beefiness in meats and adding deeper, smoky flavors. I like to experiment with different brands of espresso powder, as each brings a different degree of intensity. I have served this rub on meats to friends who hate coffee, yet they always ask for more.

2 tbsp chili powder
2 tbsp instant espresso powder
2 tbsp sweet smoked paprika
1 tbsp light brown sugar
1 tbsp onion powder
1 tbsp mild mustard powder
1 tbsp kosher salt
1 tbsp finely ground black pepper

1. Mix together all the ingredients in a small bowl. Store in an airtight container. **2.** Rub on any cut of beef and thicker pork cuts before grilling.

Moroccan Spice Rub

MAKES: about ⅓ cup • **PREP:** 10 minutes

My friend Patti travels all over the world and always brings me back a little trinket or some other treasure. One year after a trip to Morocco, she brought me an incredibly exotic and fragrant rub. I hoarded that rub, but started to panic when the container was almost empty. I spent hours trying to duplicate the flavor, my kitchen counter stacked with spices. I finally came up with a version that was as close as I could get to the one from the spice markets of Morocco.

1 tbsp ground coriander
1 tbsp kosher salt
1 tbsp regular paprika
2 tsp ground turmeric
1 tsp dehydrated sweet red pepper flakes
1 tsp finely ground black pepper
1 tsp ground cumin, toasted
1 tsp finely ground Aleppo pepper (see sidebar)
½ tsp ground ginger
½ tsp cinnamon

1. Mix together all the ingredients in a small bowl. Store in an airtight container. **2.** Rub on beef, pork, poultry and seafood or sprinkle on vegetables before grilling.

Q SAVVY

Aleppo pepper is a popular spice used in Middle Eastern cuisines. Can't find it? Substitute ancho powder.

Christo's Green Herbed Salt

MAKES: 5 to 6 cups • **PREP:** 30 minutes • **DRY:** overnight

Chef Christo Gonzales was a tough-assed New Yorker and an acclaimed chef in that city. He was also a loving father and a dear friend, and he left us all too soon. Christo was never afraid to experiment, and together we made an unstoppable grilling team, always playing to win. He used this salt (aka Christo's Magic Green Seasoning) on just about everything. Think of salt jacked up to the next level, with an added kick of herbs. It is highly addictive and adds a wonderful flavor to everyday dishes.

3 lb kosher salt, divided

1 bunch green onions, chopped

3 long sprigs fresh rosemary, leaves picked

3 sprigs fresh thyme, leaves picked

3 long sprigs fresh oregano

¼ cup finely ground black pepper

1. Place 2 cups of salt in a food processor. Add the green onions, rosemary and thyme leaves, and oregano sprigs. Pulse until a wet, green paste forms. **2.** Gradually add the rest of the salt, pulsing after each addition, until all the salt has been added. **3.** Spread the salt in an even layer on a large rimmed baking sheet. Let dry at room temperature overnight (in humid weather, this may take a little longer). **4.** The next day, break up any clumps that have formed. Mix in the pepper and store in nonmetallic airtight containers.

Smoked Salt

MAKES: 2 cups • **PREP:** 15 minutes • **COOK:** 1½ to 2 hours

Knowing how simple and inexpensive it is to make, I cringe every time I see a box of overpriced smoked salt. This is a completely customizable recipe: pick the wood you like; add herbs, if you wish (see sidebar). Share it with friends and stop buying expensive smoked salt.

Hickory, pecan, apple, mesquite or cherry wood chips

2 cups kosher salt

Q SAVVY

You can add fresh herbs to the salt for even more flavor—rosemary, thyme and chives all work well. Simply combine the herbs with the salt before spreading it out thinly in the aluminum pan.

. . . .

Change up the flavor of any rub recipe by substituting smoked salt for kosher.

1. Prepare your smoker or grill for indirect cooking and preheat it to 250°F to 275°F. Add two large handfuls of wood chips, following the instructions on page 9 for your type of smoker or grill. **2.** Spread out the kosher salt thinly in a large disposable aluminum pan. When the wood chips start to smoke, place the pan of salt on the cool side of the grill. Smoke the salt for 1½ to 2 hours, rotating the pan every 15 minutes. **3.** Remove the pan from the grill and let the salt cool to room temperature. Store in a sealed mason jar.

Kentucky Mop Sauce

MAKES: about 1¼ cups • **PREP:** 10 minutes • **COOK:** 15 to 20 minutes

One of the most spectacular sights I have ever witnessed was at the St. Mary of the Woods church picnic in Whitesville, KY. There were open-air pits loaded up with mutton that stretched almost as far as the eye could see. I was gobsmacked. At the picnic, they mopped the mutton with a savory mix and smoked it for hours. The result was dripping with delicious. Here is my version of the Whitesville mop.

¼ cup canola oil

¼ cup minced sweet white onion

½ cup Worcestershire sauce

¼ cup white vinegar

2 tsp freshly squeezed lemon juice

2 tsp packed light brown sugar

1 tsp finely ground black pepper

1 tsp hot sauce

1 tsp kosher salt

1 tsp dehydrated sweet red pepper flakes

1. Heat the oil in a medium saucepan over medium heat. Sauté the onions until softened but not browned. **2.** Add the remaining ingredients and simmer for 10 to 15 minutes. Store in an airtight container in the fridge for up to two days. **3.** Use as a mop on lamb, chicken or pork.

Q SAVVY

Mops are thinner basting sauces and a great way to add another dimension of flavor to barbecue. Use them alone on meats or in conjunction with a rub (see page 32).

Alabama White Sauce

MAKES: about 5 cups • **PREP:** 10 minutes

A barbecue sauce made with mayonnaise? Seriously? That's what you get when you visit the legendary Big Bob Gibson Bar-B-Q in Decatur, AL. Bob Gibson invented Alabama white sauce, and the chicken at the restaurant is liberally baptized with it. While I couldn't get Big Bob's recipe, my version is all sorts of fantastic and just as lip-smackingly good as everyday red barbecue sauce. I have eaten potatoes, chicken and pork slathered with this sauce. It should come with a warning: highly addictive.

3½ cups good-quality mayonnaise, such as Hellmann's or Duke's

1 cup apple cider vinegar

¼ cup light corn syrup

2 tbsp Sriracha sauce

1 tsp finely ground black pepper

1 tsp chili powder

1. Mix together all the ingredients in a large bowl. Refrigerate until ready to use. **2.** Slather on chicken during cooking, or use as a finishing sauce on pork and seafood.

Texas Mop Sauce

MAKES: about 3 cups • **PREP:** 10 minutes • **COOK:** 30 minutes

I love visiting Texas. From the ranches to the cities to the big personalities and massive hearts of the people who live there, there's nothing small about Texas. The state does beef like no other. This sauce is a great compilation of seasonings that works so well on big beef roasts and game meats.

1 bottle (12 oz/355 mL) Shiner Bock or other bock beer
½ cup apple cider vinegar
¼ cup canola oil
¼ cup Worcestershire sauce
3 tbsp Montreal Steak Spice (page 26)
2 tbsp minced garlic
2 tbsp yellow mustard
2 tbsp hot red pepper flakes
2 tbsp honey
1 tbsp coarsely ground black pepper (butcher grind)

1. Mix together all the ingredients in a medium saucepan. Simmer for 30 minutes. Store in an airtight container in the fridge for up to two days. **2.** Use as a mop on big beefy cuts of meat or game.

Q SAVVY

Use a standard barbecue mop, basting brush or even a bunch of rosemary to apply a mop sauce.

Experiment with different types of beer to change up the flavor profile of your mop sauce.

Kansas City Sweet BBQ Sauce

MAKES: about 4 cups • **PREP:** 15 minutes • **COOK:** about 15 minutes

Kansas City, MO, is full of legendary barbecue joints. When I'm there, I love grabbing some friends and making a day of trying different restaurants. This sauce is a classic of many of them, and if you are looking for an everyday barbecue sauce, this is it.

1 tbsp canola oil
2 tbsp minced white sweet onion
½ cup apple cider vinegar
2 tbsp minced garlic
2 tbsp tomato paste
2 tbsp yellow mustard
1 tbsp chili powder
2 tsp ground ginger
1 tsp chipotle powder
1 tsp kosher salt
2 cups packed dark brown sugar
1 cup ketchup
¼ cup Worcestershire sauce
2 tbsp granulated sugar

1. Heat the oil in a medium saucepan over medium heat. Sauté the onion until softened but not browned. **2.** Add the vinegar, garlic, tomato paste, mustard, chili powder, ginger, chipotle powder and salt. Simmer for 10 minutes. **3.** Add the brown sugar, ketchup, Worcestershire sauce and granulated sugar. Boil for 2 to 3 minutes, whisking often. Store in an airtight container in the fridge for up to three weeks.

Q SAVVY

Make this sauce your own by changing up the ingredients to suit your preferences. Want it sweeter? Add ¼ cup honey or molasses. Spicier? Add 2 tbsp minced canned chipotles in adobo sauce.

Diva Q Carolina Mustard BBQ Sauce

MAKES: about 2 cups • **PREP:** 10 minutes • **COOK:** about 15 minutes

I love feeding friends and family. One night I served pork with this Carolina-inspired mustard sauce. My guests were a bit skeptical, as none had tried a yellow mustard sauce before. By the end of dinner, they were all converts. They also keep asking me to make it for them again.

½ cup yellow mustard

½ cup apple cider vinegar

½ cup packed light brown sugar

¼ cup minced onion

¼ cup honey

1 tbsp Worcestershire sauce

1 tsp minced garlic

1 tsp hot sauce

½ tsp kosher salt

½ tsp chipotle powder

1. Mix together all the ingredients in a medium saucepan. Bring to a boil, whisking often. **2.** Reduce the heat and simmer, whisking occasionally, for 15 minutes. Serve on pulled pork, ribs, ham or pulled chicken. Store in an airtight container in the fridge for up to three weeks.

Q SAVVY

Sometimes it's good to get out of the barbecue rut of sweet tomato- or ketchup-based sauces, and mustard sauces are darn good eating. Sweatman's Bar-b-que in Holly Hill, SC, serves up one of the best I've ever tried.

Diva Q Competition Sauce

MAKES: about 10 cups • **PREP:** 20 minutes • **COOK:** about 25 minutes

A glossy shellac finish is what I always look for in a competition sauce, and this deep mahogany one has it in spades. The sweet sauce adds incredible color and flavor to chicken or pork. Spice it up with extra hot sauce or tone it down—either way, it's a winner.

4 cups ketchup

2 cups packed light brown sugar

2 cups apple cider vinegar

2 cups apple cider or juice

½ cup yellow mustard

½ cup honey

2 tbsp granulated garlic (see page 25)

2 tbsp granulated onion (see page 25)

2 tbsp chili powder

2 tbsp tamarind paste

1 tbsp coarsely ground black pepper (butcher grind)

1 tsp ground ginger

1 tsp hot sauce (or more to taste)

1 tsp chipotle powder

1 tsp kosher salt

½ tsp vanilla

1. Mix together all the ingredients in a large saucepan. Simmer, whisking often, until the tamarind paste has dissolved and all the ingredients are well combined, 15 to 20 minutes. **2.** Bring the sauce to a rolling boil for 5 minutes, whisking often. **3.** Remove from the heat and let cool for 10 minutes. Store in nonmetallic airtight containers in the fridge.

Q SAVVY

This recipe makes a large quantity of sauce that's perfect for canning or giving away to friends and family.

Diva Q Diablo Steak Sauce

MAKES: about 2 cups • **PREP:** 15 minutes • **COOK:** about 15 minutes

If I can't be at my grill, puttering around with ingredients in my kitchen is my next favorite thing to do. This is a quick, thrown-together-from-stuff-I-had-in-the-fridge kind of sauce. It's full of beefy, spicy goodness that can turn a plain-Jane roast or steak into something spectacular.

2 tbsp extra virgin olive oil

¼ cup minced onion

2 tbsp minced garlic

1 can (10 oz/284 mL) condensed beef consommé

¼ cup Sriracha sauce

2 tbsp Worcestershire sauce

¼ cup water

2 tbsp cornstarch

Kosher salt and finely ground black pepper to taste

1. Heat the oil in a small saucepan over medium heat. Sauté the onion and garlic until softened but not browned. **2.** Whisk in the consommé, Sriracha sauce and Worcestershire sauce. Bring to a rolling boil over high heat, whisking often. **3.** Whisk together the water and cornstarch in a small bowl until smooth. Whisk the cornstarch mixture into the sauce. Bring back to a boil, whisking constantly, until the sauce thickens. **4.** Remove from the heat and season to taste with salt and pepper. Serve with beef. Store in an airtight container in the fridge for up to two days.

Piri Piri Hot Sauce

MAKES: 5 to 6 cups • **PREP:** 20 minutes • **SOAK:** overnight • **COOK:** about 25 minutes • **AGE:** 2 weeks

I was not familiar with piri piri peppers until my friends Jen and Jeff came back from a trip to Portugal, where Jen's family has a house. Jen and Jeff share my love of food, and they brought back dried piri piri peppers for me to try. The peppers have an intense, bold heat level and are perfect for making hot sauce.

1 cup dried piri piri peppers (see sidebar)

2 cups boiling water

3 tbsp canola oil

1 cup finely chopped red onion

6 jalapeños, seeded and finely chopped

1 can (14 oz/398 mL) diced tomatoes

½ cup dehydrated sweet red pepper flakes

3 tbsp minced garlic

2 tsp granulated sugar

2 tsp kosher salt

1 cup white vinegar

1. Put the piri piri peppers in a medium glass bowl. Add the boiling water. Cover the bowl with plastic wrap and set aside overnight.
2. The next day, strain the piri piri peppers, reserving the water.
3. Heat the oil in a medium saucepan over medium heat. Sauté the onion until softened but not browned. **4.** Add 1 cup of the reserved piri piri soaking water and the jalapeños. Sauté until the jalapeños have softened. **5.** Stir in the piri piri peppers, tomatoes, red pepper flakes, garlic, sugar and salt. Remove the saucepan from the heat.
6. In a food processor, pulse the piri piri pepper mixture until smooth. Add the vinegar and pulse again until well combined.
7. Scrape the sauce into a nonmetallic container with a tightfitting lid and refrigerate for 2 weeks to let the flavors mature.

Carolina Spicy Vinegar Sauce

MAKES: 6¹/₂ cups • **PREP:** 10 minutes • **COOK:** about 5 minutes

I love North Carolina, and many of my barbecue adventures have happened there. I once did an eating tour of the state's barbecue joints that left me with cracked lips from trying so many outstanding vinegar-based sauces. It was worth every single bite. North Carolina's sauces have such a refreshing flavor profile compared to others. I love how vinegar sauces soak deep into the meat. The flecks of red pepper in this one add a mild level of spice. Pork rules in North Carolina. Buy some and try this.

4 cups apple cider vinegar

1 cup ketchup

½ cup packed light brown sugar

¼ cup finely ground tellicherry black pepper (see sidebar)

¼ cup Tabasco chipotle sauce

¼ cup good-quality kosher salt

2 tbsp dehydrated sweet red pepper flakes

2 tbsp Worcestershire sauce

1. Mix together all the ingredients in a medium saucepan. Boil for 5 minutes, whisking often to dissolve the sugar and salt. **2.** Let cool to room temperature. Serve on World Championship–Winning Pulled Pork (page 75).

Q SAVVY

Tellicherry peppercorns have a deep, rich flavor and are considered to be the finest in the world.

Jamaican Jerk Wet Rum Slather

MAKES: about 1³/₄ cups • **PREP:** 20 minutes

Long, long ago, I dated a very handsome and oh-so-flirty Jamaican guy. The relationship didn't last, but his grandma and mom were killer cooks, so I did get some great tips on Jamaican jerk dishes from his family.

½ cup minced red onion

¼ cup minced scotch bonnet peppers (with their seeds)

¼ cup finely minced jalapeños (with their seeds)

¼ cup chopped green onions

¼ cup canola oil

¼ cup Appleton Estate or other amber rum

2 tsp kosher salt

2 tsp finely ground white pepper

1½ tsp dried thyme leaves

1 tsp ground allspice

½ tsp cinnamon

¼ tsp grated nutmeg

1. Place all the ingredients in a food processor and pulse until smooth. **2.** Use as a wet rub on pork, chicken and salmon, or to marinate larger pieces of meat overnight before grilling. Store in an airtight container in the fridge for up to three days.

Q SAVVY

For milder jerk, reduce the scotch bonnets, or jack it up to hellfire level by substituting ghost peppers for the scotch bonnets.

Cherry-Chipotle BBQ Sauce

MAKES: about 5¼ cups • **PREP:** 10 minutes • **COOK:** 15 minutes

You know those times in the grocery store when you buy a bunch of something just because it's on sale? That's why one day I stood at my freezer looking at a bag of frozen sweet cherries I didn't have a need for. This sauce, with its winning combo of cherries and chipotles, was the result. Since first making it, I've been back to the store to buy many more packages of frozen cherries. Funny how things work out.

3 cups frozen sweet cherries

1 cup ketchup

½ cup packed light brown sugar

2 canned chipotles in adobo sauce

2 tbsp Worcestershire sauce

2 tbsp yellow mustard

2 tbsp freshly squeezed lemon juice

1 tbsp granulated garlic (see page 25)

1 tbsp granulated onion (see page 25)

1 tsp finely ground black pepper

1 tsp kosher salt

1. Mix together all the ingredients in a medium saucepan. Bring to a boil, stirring often. **2.** Reduce the heat and simmer for 10 to 15 minutes. Remove from the heat and let cool. **3.** In a blender or food processor, pulse the sauce until smooth. Serve with pork, chicken and game. Store in an airtight container in the fridge for up to three weeks.

Blackberry Sauce

MAKES: about 4½ cups • **PREP:** 15 minutes • **COOK:** about 20 minutes

I support farmers' markets whenever I can, and I love walking around talking to vendors. I have a serious fondness for homemade preserves, and I buy them regularly. Fruit preserves are a great start to any sauce. Just add a few other ingredients and you have a delightfully different barbecue sauce.

2 tbsp canola oil

¼ cup minced sweet white onion

2 cups blackberry preserves

1 cup ketchup

½ cup apple cider vinegar

¼ cup agave nectar

2 tbsp Dijon mustard

2 tbsp red wine vinegar

1 tsp hot sauce

½ tsp finely ground black pepper

1. Heat the oil in a medium saucepan over medium heat. Sauté the onion until softened but not browned. **2.** Add the remaining ingredients and bring to a boil, whisking often. Reduce the heat and simmer for 15 minutes, whisking occasionally. **3.** While the sauce is still warm, strain it through a fine-mesh sieve to remove the blackberry seeds. Use on pork, chicken, beef and game. Store in an airtight container in the fridge for up to three days.

Q SAVVY

Try substituting raspberry, strawberry or even apricot preserves for the blackberry and make a whole new sauce.

Apple-Beer BBQ Sauce

MAKES: about 6 cups • **PREP:** 15 minutes • **COOK:** about 25 minutes

At one of the first large competitions I entered, there was a beer garden. Not much of a shock, since beer and barbecue are a match made in heaven. What was memorable was an apple pilsner made by a Burlington, ON, brewery called Nickel Brook. The beer was light and refreshing and perfect. I immediately started thinking of recipes I could make with it. This sauce came from that wonderful first experience.

2 tbsp unsalted butter

1 cup peeled, cored and grated apple, such as Red or Golden Delicious

¼ cup finely diced white sweet onion

1 can (16 oz/473 mL) Nickel Brook Green Apple Pilsner or 2 cups hard cider

1 cup ketchup

¾ cup packed light brown sugar

½ cup apple cider

¼ cup apple cider vinegar

2 tbsp Tabasco chipotle sauce

1 tsp minced garlic

½ tsp kosher salt

½ tsp cinnamon

½ tsp granulated garlic (see page 25)

¼ tsp finely ground black pepper

¼ tsp ground allspice

1. Melt the butter in a medium saucepan over medium heat. Sauté the apple and onion until softened but not browned. **2.** Add the remaining ingredients and bring to a boil. Let boil until the sauce has reduced by about half, whisking often. **3.** Reduce the heat and simmer until the sauce has thickened, about 15 minutes. **4.** Use an immersion blender in the saucepan to purée the sauce until smooth, or, if you prefer, leave it chunky. Serve with pork and chicken. Store in an airtight container in the fridge for up to three days.

Q SAVVY

For a non-alcoholic alternative, or if you find apple beer hard to find in winter, substitute apple cider or unfiltered apple juice for the Pilsner.

Homemade Smoked Ketchup

MAKES: about 5½ cups • **PREP:** 20 minutes • **COOK:** 2½ hours

Everyone loves ketchup, and this recipe takes it to a whole new level. Smoking the tomatoes over hickory adds richness, depth and complexity while letting the tomato flavor shine. I like to use canned San Marzano tomatoes for this recipe, as fresh tomatoes never seem to break down properly. This will become a favorite condiment, I promise.

Hickory wood chips

2 cans (each 28 oz/796 mL) whole San Marzano tomatoes

1 cup canned puréed tomatoes

¾ cup packed light brown sugar

¾ cup apple cider vinegar

½ cup finely chopped white sweet onion

1 tbsp minced garlic

1 tsp celery salt

1 tsp kosher salt

1 tsp mustard powder

½ tsp finely ground black pepper

¼ tsp ground allspice

2 bay leaves

1. Prepare your smoker or grill for indirect cooking and preheat it to 225°F. Add two large handfuls of hickory chips, following the instructions on page 9 for your type of smoker or grill. **2.** Mix together all the ingredients in a large disposable aluminum pan. **3.** When the hickory chips start to smoke, place the pan containing the tomato mixture on the cool side of the grill. Smoke for 1 hour, stirring the tomato mixture every 15 minutes. **4.** Add two more large handfuls of wood chips to the smoker or grill. Smoke for an additional 1 to 1½ hours, stirring every 15 minutes, until the tomato mixture has reduced by half. **5.** Remove the aluminum pan from the grill and let the ketchup cool to room temperature. Remove the bay leaves. **6.** In a blender or food processor, purée the ketchup until smooth. Serve with everything. Store in an airtight container in the fridge for up to three weeks.

Q SAVVY

Give the smoked ketchup a boost by adding dried herbs like basil and thyme.

Orange Shrimp Lollipops (page 59)

FIRED-UP
APPETIZERS AND SHAREABLES

Kick off any party or random beers-in-the-driveway kind of
get-together with these mouthwatering, gotta-have-'em appetizers
and other little things to share.

Smoked Kale Chips

MAKES: 4 servings • **PREP:** 10 minutes • **COOK:** 25 to 30 minutes

A snack with the texture of a potato chip but the health benefits of a vegetable: how's that for a nutritional home run? My kids love these smoked kale chips and gobble them up insanely fast. I like the color contrast of using black and green kale, but you can use all one kind if you prefer.

Apple wood chips

1 small bunch green kale, separated into leaves

1 small bunch black kale, separated into leaves

3 tbsp extra virgin olive oil

2 tsp kosher salt

2 tsp finely ground black pepper

Smoked Salt to taste (page 30)

1. Prepare your smoker or grill for indirect cooking and preheat it to 250°F. Add a handful of apple chips, following the instructions on page 9 for your type of smoker or grill. **2.** Spread out the kale leaves in a single layer on a very large rimmed baking sheet. Drizzle with oil and season with salt and pepper to taste. **3.** When the wood chips start to smoke, place the baking sheet on the cool side of the grill. Smoke for 15 minutes. **4.** Turn the kale leaves over and smoke until they are bright green and just crispy but not browned, 10 to 15 minutes. **5.** Remove the baking sheet from the grill. Tip the kale leaves into a large bowl and sprinkle with smoked salt to taste.

Q SAVVY

Very thick kale leaves may take up to 1 hour to become crispy on the smoker.

Smoked Savory Nuts

MAKES: 8 servings • **PREP:** 15 minutes • **COOK:** 30 to 40 minutes

Whether you want them savory or sweet and spicy (see sidebar), these smoked nuts are simple to make and taste amazing.

Hickory wood chips

2 lb mixed unsalted nuts (almonds, pecans, peanuts)

2 tbsp clarified unsalted butter (see page 76)

1½ tsp Tabasco chipotle sauce

1½ tsp Worcestershire sauce

1 tsp toasted sesame oil

1 tsp kosher salt

1. Prepare your smoker or grill for indirect cooking and preheat it to 300°F. Add a large handful of hickory chips, following the instructions on page 9 for your type of smoker or grill. **2.** Mix together the nuts, butter, Tabasco and Worcestershire sauces and sesame oil in a medium bowl. **3.** Spread the nut mixture out in a single layer in a large disposable aluminum pan. **4.** When the chips are smoking, place the pan on the cool side of the grill. Smoke the nuts for 30 to 40 minutes, stirring them every 10 minutes. **5.** Remove the pan from the grill. Sprinkle the nuts with salt and toss well. **6.** Let the nuts cool completely, then store in an airtight container in a cool, dry place.

Q SAVVY

Sweet and Spicy Smoked Nuts

This sweeter version is great for snacking or adding to cookies, cakes or pies. Follow the recipe above, substituting 2 tbsp honey powder,* 1 tsp cinnamon and 1 tsp cayenne for the Tabasco and Worcestershire sauces, sesame oil and salt.

* Honey powder is a powdered form of honey made from dehydrated honey and fructose. It's available online or in big box stores.

Smoked Savory Nuts and Smoked Party Mix (page 46)

Smoked Party Mix
Photo on page 45

MAKES: about 32 servings • **PREP:** 15 minutes • **COOK:** 2 to 3 hours

My mom used to make this snack mix every Christmas, and I loved the intoxicating aroma as it baked. I've kept up the tradition, but put my own spin on it with the addition of a little smoke. Once it's baked, I have to hide this mix away so it actually lasts through the holidays.

2 batches Smoked Savory Nuts (page 44)

2 lb pretzel sticks

2 pkgs (each 11 oz/312 g) cheddar Goldfish

1 pkg (22 oz/620 g) Shreddies cereal

1 pkg (15 oz/425 g) plain Life cereal

1 pkg (14 oz/396 g) plain Cheerios cereal

Topping

1 cup peanut oil

1 cup clarified unsalted butter
(see page 76)

2 tbsp Worcestershire sauce

2 tsp granulated garlic (see page 25)

2 tsp granulated onion (see page 25)

2 tsp Lawry's Seasoned Salt

1. Preheat the oven to 250°F. **2.** Combine the nuts, pretzel sticks, Goldfish, Shreddies, Life cereal and Cheerios in a very large bowl. **3.** Whisk together all the topping ingredients in a medium bowl. Drizzle the oil mixture over the snack mix and toss gently to coat well. **4.** Spread out the snack mix on 4 large rimmed baking sheets or in 2 large disposable aluminum pans. **5.** Bake until crisp and fragrant, 2 to 3 hours, stirring every 15 minutes. **6.** Let cool completely, then store in an airtight container in a cool, dry place.

Chipotle Devilled Eggs with Pig Candy
MAKES: 24 eggs • **PREP:** 30 minutes

Creamy devilled eggs are just pure old-fashioned goodness. The most fiddly part of this recipe is the shelling of the eggs, but otherwise it's a breeze to make, and the chipotles and Pig Candy make this classic appetizer truly extraordinary.

12 hard-cooked large eggs, peeled

½ cup good-quality mayonnaise, such as Hellmann's or Duke's

2 tsp minced canned chipotles in adobo sauce

½ tsp sweet smoked paprika

Kosher salt and finely ground black pepper to taste

4 slices Pig Candy, finely chopped (page 110)

1. Cut the eggs in half lengthwise and carefully remove the yolks to a bowl. Set the whites aside on a serving platter. **2.** Mash the yolks until smooth. Add the mayonnaise, chipotles, paprika, and salt and pepper to taste. Mix until smooth. **3.** Spoon the yolk mixture into a piping bag. Pipe the yolk mixture into the egg white cavities, dividing evenly. **4.** Top each devilled egg with a sprinkling of Pig Candy.

Q SAVVY

Ever notice that, at a picnic or party, the devilled eggs are always the first appetizer to disappear? Make a few batches for your next bash.

Chipotle Devilled Eggs and Perfectly Pink Potato Salad (page 225)

Cold-Smoked Cheddar–Pimento Cheese

MAKES: 6 to 8 servings • **PREP:** 15 minutes • **CHILL:** at least 2 hours

I am a pimento cheese addict. One taste of this creamy, smoky spread and you will be searching—and I mean searching—for anything to put it on. Crackers, bread, burgers, sausages . . . you name it, pimento cheese makes it perfect.

1 lb shredded cold-smoked cheddar (page 18)

1 jar (7 oz/200 mL) pimentos, drained and finely chopped

2 tbsp finely grated sweet white onion

½ tsp finely ground black pepper

½ tsp chipotle powder

1 cup good-quality mayonnaise, such as Hellmann's or Duke's

Kosher salt to taste

1. Mix together the cheddar, pimentos, onion, pepper and chipotle powder in a large bowl. **2.** Stir in the mayonnaise, mashing the mixture with a fork until it is relatively smooth. Season with salt to taste. **3.** Scrape the mixture into a serving bowl. Cover and refrigerate for at least 2 hours to allow the flavors to develop.

Killer Guacamole

MAKES: 6 servings • **PREP:** 15 minutes • **STAND:** 20 minutes

Guacamole always seemed kind of blah to me, lacking both flavor and texture. Then, on a trip to Mexico, I got chatting to a lady called Rosario. Between her broken English and my horrific Spanish, she walked me through her recipe for guacamole. Now I get guac and have been making Rosario's recipe ever since. At least once a year, I take a batch to *The Marilyn Denis Show* because it's my Marilyn-loves-it guacamole.

2 large ripe avocados

2 limes, zested and juiced

3 roma tomatoes, cored, seeded and finely chopped

½ cup finely minced red onion

¼ cup finely chopped fresh cilantro

½ tsp kosher salt

½ tsp finely ground black pepper

½ tsp chipotle powder

1. Peel and pit the avocados. Mash them in a large bowl with the lime zest and juice. **2.** Fold in the remaining ingredients. Let the guacamole stand at room temperature for 20 minutes before serving.

Q SAVVY

Before storing leftover guacamole in the fridge, press a sheet of plastic wrap directly on the surface of the guacamole to help prevent the avocado from browning.

Want a grilled guac? Pit the avocados and drizzle with olive oil. Grill, flesh-side down, on a medium-high (375°F to 450°F) grill until charred.

Cold-Smoked Cheddar-Pimento Cheese

Macedonian Roasted Red Pepper and Eggplant Spread

MAKES: 6 to 8 servings • **PREP:** 1 hour • **COOK:** about 30 minutes

I have friends from Macedonia. Of all the dishes they've introduced me to over the years, the one that stands out is this spread, known as *ajvar* (pronounced "ag-var"). Ajvar is one of the most versatile dishes: serve it as a dip, toss it with pasta or serve with Chevaps (page 61) and feta cheese. In the summer, they grill entire bushels of red peppers to make huge quantities of ajvar. Here's my scaled-down version of the family recipe.

5 sweet red peppers

2 medium eggplants

½ cup sunflower oil

6 cloves Smoked Garlic (page 15)

3 tbsp apple cider vinegar

1 tsp Vegeta (see sidebar) or Mrs. Dash Original Blend

1. Prepare your grill for direct cooking and preheat it to medium-high (375°F to 450°F). **2.** Grill the peppers and eggplants, turning often, until the peppers are blackened all over and the eggplants are charred and very soft. The peppers will take 10 to 15 minutes, the eggplants about 25 minutes. **3.** Transfer the peppers to a large bowl and cover tightly with plastic wrap. Place the eggplants on a baking sheet. Set the peppers and eggplants aside until they're cool enough to handle. **4.** Peel the charred skin from the peppers. Remove the stems, seeds and membranes. Chop the peppers coarsely and place in a food processor. **5.** Split the eggplants in half. Scoop the flesh out of the skins and add to the food processor. **6.** Add the oil, smoked garlic, vinegar and Vegeta to the food processor. Pulse the mixture until smooth. Scrape the ajvar into a large bowl. Serve at room temperature or cold.

Q SAVVY

For a spicy version of ajvar, substitute hot peppers for some or all of the sweet peppers.

. . . .

Vegeta is an eastern European seasoning blend. Look for it in European grocery stores and larger supermarkets.

Grilled Mango-Poblano Salsa

MAKES: 4 servings • **PREP:** 30 minutes • **COOK:** 3 to 4 minutes • **STAND:** 30 minutes

I get bored with tomato salsa. In this grilled mango-poblano combo, the sweet starchiness of the mangos is perfectly offset by the smokiness and spice of the poblanos. The longer you grill or smoke poblanos, the more their heat is tempered. Serve this with your favorite chips or spoon over tacos, nachos or steak.

Canola oil for oiling

2 ripe mangos, peeled, pitted and sliced lengthwise

1 poblano, seeded and halved

2 jalapeños, seeded and minced

1 sweet red pepper, seeded and minced

2 limes, zested and juiced

¼ cup minced red onion

2 tsp extra virgin olive oil

1 tsp grated fresh ginger

1 bunch fresh cilantro, leaves picked and finely chopped

Kosher salt and finely ground black pepper to taste

Cilantro leaves and lime slices for garnish

1. Prepare the grill for direct cooking and preheat it to medium-high (375°F to 450°F). Generously oil the grill grates. **2.** Grill the mango slices and poblano, turning often, until the mango slices are lightly charred and just tender and the poblano is tender and its skin has blistered, 3 to 4 minutes. **3.** Remove the mango slices and poblano from the grill. Cube the mango. Chop the poblano finely. **4.** Gently stir together the mango, poblano and remaining ingredients in a medium bowl. Let stand for 30 minutes before serving. **5.** Garnish the salsa with cilantro leaves and lime slices.

Mint Limeade

2 cups freshly squeezed lime juice (about 10 limes)

2 cups lime-flavored sparkling water

¼ cup packed fresh mint leaves

2 limes, thinly sliced

1 tbsp finely grated lime zest

Crushed ice

Lime wedges for garnish

Simple Mint Syrup

1½ cups granulated sugar

1½ cups water

1 small bunch mint, leaves picked

MAKES: 8 servings • **PREP:** 15 minutes • **COOK:** 10 minutes

This is my daughter Lexi's favorite summer drink and the perfect pairing for salsa and chips. For an adult version, add tequila or vodka to taste.

1. Mix together all the mint syrup ingredients in a small saucepan. Bring to a boil, stirring to dissolve the sugar. **2.** Reduce the heat and simmer for 10 minutes. **3.** Remove the saucepan from the heat and let the syrup cool (the longer the syrup steeps, the stronger the mint flavor). **4.** Strain through a fine-mesh sieve, discarding the mint. Refrigerate until chilled. (The mint syrup will keep for weeks in the fridge.) **5.** Mix together the mint syrup, lime juice, sparkling water, mint leaves, sliced limes and lime zest in a large pitcher. **6.** Pour into glasses over crushed ice and garnish with lime wedges.

Smoked Cheddar–Jalapeño Cornbread Bites

MAKES: 18 to 20 bites • **PREP:** 20 minutes • **COOK:** 15 to 20 minutes

These are yummy, buttery, cheesy mouthfuls. Trust me: they'll barely make it out of the oven before everyone gobbles them up. The bites also make a great side for grilled sausage or steak.

1 cup all-purpose flour

¾ cup cornmeal

2 tbsp granulated sugar

2½ tsp baking powder

½ tsp chili powder

¾ tsp table salt

1 cup whole milk

2 eggs, beaten

¼ cup unsalted butter, melted

1 cup shredded cold-smoked cheddar
  (page 18)

2 jalapeños, seeded and minced

Herbed Garlic Butter

¼ cup salted butter, melted

2 tsp finely chopped fresh flat-leaf
  parsley

1 tsp finely chopped fresh chives

½ tsp garlic powder

1. Preheat the oven to 400°F. Lightly grease a large baking sheet. **2.** Whisk together the flour, cornmeal, sugar, baking powder, chili powder and salt in a medium bowl. Set aside. **3.** Whisk together the milk, eggs and melted butter. Stir in the cheese and jalapeños. **4.** Add the milk mixture all at once to the flour mixture. Stir just until the dry ingredients are moistened (don't overmix). **5.** Using a 1-inch ice-cream scoop, drop portions of the batter, 1 inch apart, onto the prepared baking sheet. **6.** Bake until a toothpick inserted in one of the bites comes out clean, 15 to 20 minutes. **7.** While the bites are baking, mix together all the garlic butter ingredients in a small bowl. **8.** As soon as the bites come out of the oven, brush them with the garlic butter. Serve warm.

Q SAVVY

You can bake on many grills (especially pellet grills) using the indirect method of cooking—so experiment with your grill capabilities! I'd recommend starting at 350°F and adjusting the temperature according to your grill type and the type of baking you are doing (each grill is unique so 350°F may be enough on one grill but not enough on another). As a general rule, add at least 15–20% additional cooking time to the recipe and check your baking frequently.

Grilled Prosciutto, Olive and Mozzarella Pizza

MAKES: 6 to 8 servings • **PREP:** 20 minutes • **REST:** 1 hour • **COOK:** about 8 minutes

Few suppers taste finer—or are easier to fix—than a wood- or charcoal-grilled pizza. I always have pizza dough in the freezer all ready for family pizza night. The dough doesn't take long to thaw, and making pizza is a great way to use up all those little bits of leftovers you might have in your fridge. For the best homemade pizza, check out my Pizza Pointers on page 57.

1 lb pizza dough

½ cup cornmeal for dusting

Canola oil for oiling (optional)

¾ cup Macedonian Roasted Red Pepper and Eggplant Spread (page 50)

1 cup shredded fresh mozzarella

½ cup pitted black olives, sliced

4 oz thinly sliced prosciutto

10 drained, oil-packed sundried tomatoes, sliced

1 small bunch fresh flat-leaf parsley, leaves picked and finely chopped

Kosher salt and finely ground black pepper to taste

One hour before grilling the pizza, remove the pizza dough from the refrigerator.

To cook on a Big Green Egg (see page 260): 1. Prepare the grill for indirect cooking. Place a pizza stone on the grill grate and preheat the grill to 600°F. **2.** Roll out the pizza dough to a 14-inch round. Dust a pizza peel with cornmeal and place the pizza dough on it. **3.** Spread the dough with the eggplant spread. Top with mozzarella, olives, prosciutto, tomatoes and parsley. Sprinkle with salt and pepper to taste. **4.** Slide the pizza onto the pizza stone and grill for 4 minutes. Rotate the pizza and grill until the edges are lightly browned and the toppings are bubbling, 2 to 3 minutes. **5.** Slide the pizza peel under the pizza and remove it from the grill.

To cook on a charcoal grill: 1. Prepare the grill for direct cooking and preheat it to medium-high (375°F to 450°F), 10 to 15 minutes. **2.** Roll out the pizza dough to a 14-inch round. Lightly oil both sides of the dough if cooking on a charcoal grill. **3.** Place the dough directly on the grill and grill for 2 to 3 minutes with the lid closed. **4.** Dust a pizza peel with cornmeal. Remove the dough from the grill and flip it onto the pizza peel so the grilled side faces up. **5.** Add the toppings as for the Big Green Egg instructions. Slide the pizza back onto the grill. Close the lid and grill the pizza until the edges are lightly browned and the toppings are bubbling, about 3 minutes. **6.** Slide the pizza peel under the pizza and remove it from the grill.

Grilled Smoked Sausage, Garlic and Provolone Pizza

MAKES: 6 to 8 servings • **PREP:** 20 minutes • **REST:** 1 hour • **COOK:** about 8 minutes

1 lb pizza dough

½ cup cornmeal for dusting

Canola oil for oiling (optional)

2 tbsp extra virgin olive oil

1 tsp Diva Q Pork and Chicken Rub (page 24)

8 oz thinly sliced Bacon-Wrapped Sausage Fatty (page 118)

½ cup sliced grilled sweet pepper

6 cloves Smoked Garlic (page 15), minced

¾ cup shredded provolone

¼ cup freshly grated Parmesan

1. Prepare the grill and dough as described in the Grilled Prosciutto, Olive and Mozzarella Pizza recipe (page 55). **2.** Brush the pizza dough with olive oil. Sprinkle with the rub. **3.** Top with the sausage fatty, sweet pepper, minced garlic and provolone. Grill as described on page 55. **4.** Remove the pizza from the grill and sprinkle with Parmesan.

Grilled Tuscan Chicken, Pepper and Goat Cheese Pizza

MAKES: 6 to 8 servings • **PREP:** 20 minutes • **REST:** 1 hour • **COOK:** about 8 minutes

1 lb pizza dough

½ cup cornmeal for dusting

Canola oil for oiling (optional)

1 cup Diva Q Competition Sauce (page 33)

2 cups shredded meat from Herbed Tuscan Bricked Chicken (page 155)

1 grilled sweet red pepper, seeded and cut into thin strips

1 grilled sweet yellow pepper, seeded and cut into thin strips

1 small red onion, very thinly sliced

1½ tsp dehydrated sweet red pepper flakes

½ cup freshly grated Parmesan

8 oz goat cheese, crumbled

2 cups lightly packed arugula leaves

Extra virgin olive oil for drizzling

1. Prepare the grill and dough as described in the Grilled Prosciutto, Olive and Mozzarella Pizza recipe (page 55), but divide the dough in half and form into two 9-inch thin-crust pizza crusts, crimping the edges of each as you would a pie. **2.** Spread the pizza dough with sauce, dividing evenly. **3.** Top with the chicken, sweet peppers and onion. Sprinkle with the red pepper flakes, then the Parmesan and goat cheese. Grill as described on page 55. **4.** Remove the pizzas from the grill. Scatter with arugula and drizzle with olive oil. Let stand for 2 minutes before serving.

Pizza Pointers

For pizzeria-worthy pizza at home, follow these simple steps:

- Make sure the grill grates are super clean.
- Always oil the grill grates and, if you are not using a pizza stone, oil the pizza crust, too.
- If using a pizza stone, place it on the grill before you light the grill so the stone heats up along with the grill.
- Whether you make your own pizza dough or use store-bought, make sure you let it rest before forming the pizzas (this makes stretching the dough easier).
- Prep all your ingredients before you head to the grill.
- Dust the pizza peel with cornmeal to prevent the dough from sticking.
- Thinly slice any raw vegetables for toppings, or grill larger pieces in advance.
- Close the lid of the grill as soon as you've added the pizza toppings.
- Keep a close eye on your pizza during grilling. Rotate it 90 degrees halfway through, if necessary, to evenly crisp the edges.
- Don't worry if your dough droops a little between the grates; as long as your grill is hot enough, the dough will firm up quickly.
- If making several pizzas, brush the pizza stone well after cooking each one.

Orange-Shrimp Lollipops
Photo on page 40

MAKES: 36 lollipops • **PREP:** 30 minutes • **COOK:** about 10 minutes

It's funny how recipes come about sometimes. While getting ready for a party once, I discovered that one of the packages of shrimp I'd bought had gone bad. With no time to run to the store, I had to come up with an appetizer using just half the shrimp. I had a bowl of navel oranges on the counter, so I paired the two and came up with these lollipops. They were such a hit, I now serve them at all my parties. These work well with grapefruit slices, too.

36 large shrimp, peeled and deveined

6 large navel oranges, cut into ¼-inch rounds

36 small soaked bamboo skewers

¼ cup Cajun Rub (page 25)

Glaze

1 cup sweet chili sauce

½ cup apple jelly

2 tbsp hot sauce

1 tbsp sweet red pepper flakes

1. Place 1 shrimp on an orange slice. Thread onto a skewer, attaching the shrimp securely. Repeat with the remaining shrimp, orange slices and skewers. **2.** Lightly sprinkle the shrimp with Cajun Rub. Set aside. **3.** Mix together all the glaze ingredients in a small saucepan. Bring to a simmer over medium heat, stirring until the jelly melts. Remove the saucepan from the heat and set aside. **4.** Prepare your grill for direct cooking and preheat it to medium-high (375°F to 450°F). **5.** Grill the shrimp, without flipping, until they are just about to turn opaque, 6 to 7 minutes. **6.** Brush the shrimp generously with the glaze and grill for 2 minutes. Serve immediately.

Shrimp-Stuffed Mushroom Bites

MAKES: 24 bites • **PREP:** 30 minutes • **COOK:** 45 to 60 minutes

No one can resist these mouthwatering little bites of deliciousness. Mushrooms teamed with shrimp and cheese? What's not to like? If you prefer, swap out the shrimp for crab or lobster meat.

8 oz herb-and-chive cream cheese

3 tbsp freshly grated Parmesan

2 tsp Diva Q Pork and Chicken Rub (page 24)

24 cremini mushrooms, cleaned and stems removed

24 small shrimp, peeled and deveined (about 1 lb)

2 jalapeños, seeded and thinly sliced

Hickory wood chips

1. Mix together the cream cheese, Parmesan and Diva Q rub in a small bowl. **2.** Fill the cavity of each mushroom cap with the cream cheese mixture, dividing evenly. Top each mushroom cap with 1 shrimp and a slice of jalapeño. **3.** Prepare your smoker or grill for indirect cooking and preheat it to 250°F. Add a handful of hickory wood chips, following the instructions on page 9 for your type of smoker or grill. **4.** When the chips start to smoke, place the mushroom caps on the cool side of the grill. Smoke the mushroom caps until the cheese is bubbling and the shrimp are opaque, 45 to 60 minutes. Serve immediately.

Q SAVVY

Chevaps are perfect party food, and this recipe makes a big batch, but you can grill them in advance and freeze them. To serve, thaw the chevaps, then reheat on the grill or in the oven.

Chevaps

MAKES: 40 to 50 sausages • PREP: 45 minutes CHILL: overnight • COOK: 12 to 15 minutes

Chevap is a nickname for a type of skinless Macedonian sausage called *cevapcic* (pronounced "che-vap-chich"). The first time I had chevaps was at my in-laws', and I loved the blend of pork, beef and spices. My father-in-law (who doesn't let anyone but him near the grill) buys his chevaps, but I've been playing around with my own recipe and they are super easy to make. The baking soda gives the sausages their tender texture, so take care when flipping them on the grill.

5 lb ground pork

5 lb ground beef (80% lean, 20% fat)

2 cups Italian-seasoned bread crumbs

1½ cups Macedonian Roasted Red Pepper and Eggplant Spread (page 50)

1 medium onion, minced

2 eggs

3 tbsp baking soda

3 tbsp minced garlic

2 tbsp dried parsley leaves

2 tbsp kosher salt

1½ tbsp ground dried porcini mushrooms

1½ tbsp sweet smoked paprika

1½ tbsp finely ground black pepper

1 tsp ground allspice

Canola oil for oiling

Additional Macedonian Roasted Red Pepper and Eggplant Spread (page 50) to serve

Crumbled feta cheese to serve

1. Place the pork, beef, bread crumbs, eggplant spread, onion, eggs, baking soda, garlic, parsley, salt, ground porcinis, paprika, pepper and allspice in a very large bowl. Mix the ingredients until thoroughly combined. **2.** Using a 3-ounce ice-cream scoop, scoop out portions of the meat mixture onto a large parchment-lined baking sheet. Form each portion into a finger-length sausage. **3.** Cover the baking sheet tightly with plastic wrap. Chill the sausages overnight until firm. **4.** Prepare your grill for direct cooking and preheat it to medium-high (375°F to 450°F). Lightly oil the grill grates. **5.** Grill the sausages in batches, turning occasionally, until the internal temperature reaches 160°F, 12 to 15 minutes. **6.** Serve with additional eggplant spread and feta cheese.

Diva Q Smokin' Caesar

½ cup clamato juice

2 oz Tito's or your favorite vodka

4 dashes Tabasco chipotle sauce

3 dashes Worcestershire sauce

Kosher salt and finely ground black pepper to taste

Ice

Diva Q Pork and Chicken Rub (page 24)

1 large shrimp, peeled, deveined and grilled

1 slice Pig Candy (page 110)

1 lime wedge

MAKES: 1 serving • PREP: 10 minutes

Chevaps and this spicy Caesar are a marriage made in heaven.

1. Combine the clamato juice, vodka, Tabasco and Worcestershire sauces and salt and pepper to taste in a cocktail shaker. Add ice and shake vigorously. **2.** Rim a large mason jar with Diva Q rub and add more ice. Strain the cocktail into the jar. **3.** Garnish with the shrimp, Pig Candy and lime wedge.

Smoked Sausage–Stuffed Poblanos

MAKES: 4 servings • **PREP:** 30 minutes • **COOK:** about 1½ hours

The original recipe for these stuffed peppers came from leftovers in the fridge, but they were so good, we make them on purpose now. Poblanos are mild peppers, and their generous size makes them easier to stuff than jalapeños. Ice-cold beer is a must with these.

1¼ lb sweet or hot Italian sausage, casings removed and sausage crumbled

1 sweet white onion, finely chopped

2 ears corn, grilled and kernels removed (page 194)

1 can (4½ oz/127 mL) chopped green chilies, drained

1 tbsp Diva Q Pork and Chicken Rub (page 24)

Hickory wood chips

4 poblanos (4 to 5 inches long)

1 cup shredded cold-smoked mozzarella (page 18)

1. Fry the sausage in a medium skillet over medium heat until almost cooked, breaking up any large pieces of sausage. **2.** Add the onion. Sauté until the onion is starting to soften but is not browned, about 5 minutes. **3.** Remove the skillet from the heat and let cool slightly. Stir in the corn, chilies and Diva Q rub. **4.** Prepare your smoker or grill for indirect cooking and preheat it to 275°F. Add a handful of hickory chips, following the instructions on page 9 for your type of smoker or grill. **5.** Make a cut lengthwise in one side of each poblano to create a pocket. Carefully remove the seeds from each poblano. Rinse the poblanos, then shake out any excess water. **6.** Carefully fill each poblano with the sausage mixture, dividing evenly. **7.** When the chips start to smoke, place the poblanos on the cool side of the grill. Smoke until the poblanos start to soften, 45 to 60 minutes. (For a very smoky flavor, replenish the wood chips by adding another handful after 30 minutes.) **8.** Top the poblanos with mozzarella, dividing evenly. Smoke until the cheese has melted, about 20 minutes. Serve immediately.

Grilled Greek Lamb Chops

MAKES: 4 servings • **PREP:** 20 minutes • **COOK:** 4 to 7 minutes

I am the first to admit that lamb isn't my favorite meat. But one day I came across some inexpensive thin-cut lamb shoulder-blade chops and decided to give them a try. They were so juicy and quick to cook, they became a family favorite. Serve them as (messy) finger food or for a speedy weeknight supper.

1 large lemon, zested and juiced

2 tbsp Greek Rub (page 28)

3 cloves Smoked Garlic (page 15), smashed

Kosher salt and finely ground black pepper to taste

8 thin-cut (½-inch) lamb shoulder-blade chops

Ken's Green Sauce (page 179)

1. Mix together the lemon zest and juice, Greek Rub, garlic, and salt and pepper to taste in a small bowl. **2.** Spread the mixture over both sides of each lamb chop. Set aside. **3.** Prepare your grill for direct cooking and preheat it to medium-high (375°F to 450°F). **4.** Grill the lamb chops, turning once, until lightly charred and the internal temperature reaches 125°F for medium-rare, 4 to 7 minutes. **5.** Remove the lamb chops from the grill and serve with Ken's Green Sauce.

Q SAVVY

If you can find them, lamb ribs are a great substitute for lamb shoulder-blade chops. Follow the recipe, but grill the ribs indirect for 3 to 4 hours, until the fat has rendered and the meat has become tender.

Smoked Scotch Eggs

MAKES: 8 scotch eggs • **PREP:** 30 minutes • **COOK:** about 1 hour

I think any day I can smoke sausage is a good day, so it made sense to treat classic sausage-wrapped Scotch eggs to a touch of smoke.

8 small eggs

Cherry wood chips

2 lb sweet or hot Italian sausage, casings removed

¼ cup Diva Q Pork and Chicken Rub (page 24)

1 cup Diva Q Competition Sauce (page 33)

Q SAVVY

Scotch teamed with Smoked Scotch Eggs? Awesome.

1. Gently lower the eggs into a saucepan of boiling water. Boil for 5 minutes, then immediately transfer the eggs to a bowl of ice water. When the eggs are cool, peel off the shells. **2.** Prepare your smoker or grill for indirect cooking and preheat it to 225°F to 250°F. Add a handful of cherry chips, following the instructions on page 9 for your type of smoker or grill. **3.** Divide the sausage into 8 equal portions. Mold a portion of sausage around each egg to cover it completely, sealing the edges well. Season the sausage-wrapped eggs with Diva Q rub. **4.** When the chips start to smoke, place the eggs on the cool side of the grill. Smoke until the internal temperature of the sausage layer reaches 155°F, 45 to 60 minutes. Replenish the wood chips by adding another handful after 30 minutes. **5.** Glaze the eggs all over with the sauce. Smoke until the sauce is set, about 10 minutes. Remove the eggs from the grill and serve warm.

Buckner Brothers' Kentucky Brown Mouthwash

Crushed ice

3 oz bourbon, such as Maker's Mark or Woodford Reserve

2 tbsp Simple Mint Syrup (page 51)

Mint sprig for garnish

MAKES: 1 serving • **PREP:** 3 minutes

The Buckner Brothers team, led by Elliot and Brian Buckner, from Virginia and New York respectively, is a serious contender in competition barbecue. The Buckners, often referred to as the frat boys of the barbecue world, always travel with their so-called Brown Bar, a veritable brown liquor buffet. Their signature "mouthwash" is perfect with the Scotch eggs.

1. Fill a glass with crushed ice. **2.** Add the bourbon and mint syrup and stir to combine. **3.** Garnish with mint.

Smoked Pumpkin Soup

MAKES: 8 to 10 servings • **PREP:** 30 minutes • **COOK:** about 2½ hours

Pumpkins are much more than a jack-o'-lantern waiting to happen. Smoking a pumpkin brings out its natural sweetness and adds a whole new level of savory richness to this velvety soup. If you're pressed for time, you can smoke the pumpkin a couple days in advance, then refrigerate the flesh for when you're ready to make the soup. The smoked pumpkin seeds are hard to resist, but try to save a few for garnishing the soup.

Hickory wood chips

1 pumpkin (about 4 lb)

2 tbsp canola oil

Kosher salt and finely ground black
    pepper to taste

2 tbsp unsalted butter

1 medium white onion, finely diced

4 cups chicken stock

1 cup whipping (heavy) cream

2 tbsp fresh thyme leaves

½ tsp cinnamon

Smoked pumpkin seeds and crumbled
    cooked bacon (optional)

Q SAVVY

For a fall dinner, I like to serve this soup in mini pumpkins.

1. Prepare your smoker or grill for indirect cooking and preheat it to 250°F. Add a handful of hickory chips, following the instructions on page 9 for your type of smoker or grill. **2.** Cut the pumpkin into quarters. Remove the seeds and set aside. Coat the flesh of the pumpkin with canola oil and season with salt and pepper to taste. **3.** Place the pumpkin on the cool side of the grill and smoke until the pumpkin is soft, 1½ to 2 hours. Replenish the wood chips by adding a handful every 30 minutes while the pumpkin smokes. **4.** Meanwhile, spread the pumpkin seeds out on a smoking mat (see page 264) or disposable aluminum pan. Place on the cool side of the grill and grill until toasted and crunchy, about 1 hour. **5.** Remove the pumpkin from the grill; when it is cool enough to handle, remove the flesh from the skin and chop coarsely. Set the pumpkin flesh and smoked pumpkin seeds aside. **6.** Melt the butter in a large pot over medium heat. Sauté the onion until softened but not browned. **7.** Add the pumpkin flesh, stock, cream, thyme and cinnamon to the pot. Bring to a boil over high heat. Reduce the heat to medium-low and simmer, uncovered, for 30 minutes. **8.** Using an immersion blender in the pot, purée the soup until smooth. Season with salt and pepper to taste. Serve sprinkled with smoked pumpkin seeds and bacon, if using.

SLING YOUR MEAT

Lip-Smacking Ribs (page 91)

PRAISE
THE PIG!

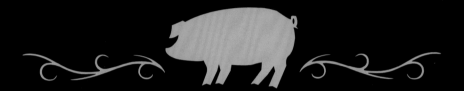

Magic happens when pork hits the grill. From chops to roasts
to ribs, these recipes will take you to pork nirvana.

Char Siu (Chinese Barbecued Pork)

MAKES: 12 servings • **PREP:** 30 minutes • **MARINATE:** overnight cook 1½ hours

I think everyone has a favorite Chinese joint. You know the type I mean. It might look a little sketchy but makes the best soup, pork, whatever. There's a Chinese restaurant in Toronto that serves the best char siu I've ever had. The gorgeous deep red-meat has addictive flavors of five-spice powder, ginger and sesame and the chewy texture I look for in good char siu. I like using a boneless pork butt for this recipe because its fat adds flavor. Seriously. Pork fat: always a good idea.

1 boneless pork butt (about 8 lb)
Cherry wood chips

Marinade
1 cup hoisin sauce
¾ cup mushroom-flavored soy sauce
½ cup honey
½ cup Sriracha sauce
½ cup dry sherry
2 tbsp minced garlic
2 tbsp minced fresh ginger
2 tbsp granulated sugar
2 tbsp umami paste (see sidebar)
1 tbsp chili oil
1 tbsp toasted sesame oil
1 tbsp five-spice powder

1. Trim any excess fat and membrane from the pork butt. Slice the pork into ¼-inch slices. Place the pork in a large resealable freezer bag. 2. Mix together all the marinade ingredients in a medium bowl. Add half of the marinade to the bag, turning to coat the pork. Seal the bag and refrigerate overnight. Refrigerate the remaining marinade. 3. Prepare your smoker or grill for indirect cooking and preheat it to 275°F. Add a handful of cherry chips, following the instructions on page 9 for your type of smoker or grill. 4. Remove the pork slices from the bag, discarding the marinade in the bag. 5. When the chips start to smoke, place the pork slices in a single layer on the cool side of the grill. Smoke the pork until the internal temperature reaches 155°F to 160°F, about 1½ hours. Glaze the pork every 15 minutes with the reserved marinade and add another handful of wood chips every 30 minutes while the pork smokes. 6. Remove the char siu from the grill, tent loosely with foil and let rest for 15 minutes before serving.

Q SAVVY

I like to throw themed dinner parties, and this recipe is always a huge favorite when I have a Chinese night. Accompany the pork with sticky rice and grilled bok choy, or serve it over miso soup for a power-packed bowl of happiness.

Umami—known as the fifth taste, after sweet, salty, sour and bitter—is like a flavor bomb and can add a punch to almost any dish. Look for umami paste in the condiments section of larger supermarkets or specialty grocery stores.

Q SAVVY

My kids love pulled pork on just about anything—even breakfast eggs. Pulled pork is super versatile and can be used in any recipe that calls for ground beef. For tips on freezing pulled pork, see page 77.

JACK DANIEL

23rd Annual Jack Daniel's
World Championship Invitational Barbecue
1st Place – "Jack Daniel's Pork"
2011 Lynchburg, Tennessee

World Championship–Winning Pulled Pork

MAKES: 20 to 30 servings • **PREP:** 45 minutes • **CHILL:** 4 hours • **COOK:** 8 to 10 hours • **REST:** 2 hours

This is it: the recipe that won my team the Jack Daniel's World Pork Championship in 2011. It was one of the best jaw-dropping-holy-crap-we-did-it moments in the team's history. We'd already placed first in six pork competitions in 2011. That the Jack was our seventh was a wonderful coincidence, Jack Daniel's whiskey being known as Old No. 7 Brand. Needless to say, we raised many toasts to Jasper—the original Jack Daniel's real name—that night. For more information on Butcher BBQ and Smoky Mountain Smokers products, see page 265.

2 bone-in pork butts (each 10 to 12 lb)
Hickory wood chips
Oak wood chips

Competition Pork Injection

1½ cups pineapple juice
¾ cup Butcher BBQ Pork Injection
¼ cup packed light brown sugar

Rub

1½ cups Butcher BBQ Honey Rub
1 cup Butcher BBQ Premium Rub
½ cup Smoky Mountain Smokers Chipotle BBQ Seasoning

Spritz

2 cups apple juice
2 tbsp MSG

Wrap

2 cups packed light brown sugar
1½ cups clarified unsalted butter (see sidebar)
1½ cups apple juice
½ cup Tabasco chipotle sauce
½ cup Butcher BBQ Honey Rub, finely ground

Sauce

Diva Q Competition Sauce (page 33)

To Serve

Butcher BBQ Honey Rub to taste
Additional Diva Q Competition Sauce
Buns and slaw

1. Trim the tops of the pork butts of excess fat, leaving the bottom fat caps intact. Refrigerate the pork butts. **2.** Whisk together all the injection ingredients in a medium bowl until the sugar has dissolved. Set the injection aside for 1 hour before filling the injector. **3.** Place each pork butt in a 2-gallon resealable freezer bag. Inject half of the injection into each pork butt, injecting the butts every ½ inch. **4.** Rub each pork butt in its bag generously with half of the Honey Rub, half of the Premium Rub and half of the Chipotle BBQ Seasoning. Seal the bags and refrigerate the pork butts for 4 hours. **5.** Mix together the spritz ingredients and pour into a spray bottle. **6.** Prepare your smoker or grill for indirect cooking and preheat it to 225°F to 250°F. Add a small handful each of hickory and oak chips, following the instructions on page 9 for your type of smoker or grill. **7.** When the wood chips start to smoke, place the pork butts on the cool side of the grill. Smoke the pork butts until the internal temperature of each reaches 165°F to 170°F and they are a deep reddish mahogany, 6 to 7 hours. Replenish the wood chips by adding a handful of each every hour while the pork butts smoke. **8.** Check the pork butts every 30 minutes. If their surfaces seem dry, spray them with the spritz. The surfaces of the pork butts should be moist but not dripping. **9.** After 6 or 7 hours, place each pork butt in a disposable aluminum pan. (Leave the grill on.) **10.** Sprinkle each pork butt with half of the brown sugar, half of the clarified butter, half of the apple juice, half of the Tabasco and half of the Honey Rub. Cover each pan with heavy-duty foil, sealing it tightly. **11.** Return the pans to the cool side of the grill and grill until the internal temperature of each pork butt reaches 200°F and the bone can be pulled out easily, 2 to 3 hours. Remove the pan from the grill. **12.** Strain the pan juices through a fine-mesh sieve. Add the strained pan juices to the Diva Q sauce and whisk thoroughly. Glaze each pork butt with the sauce. **13.** Cover the pans with plastic wrap and a double layer of foil. Place the pans in a cooler or a very large plastic container and cover them with towels. Let the pork butts rest for 2 hours. **14.** To serve, pull the pork butts into large chunks, discarding any fat and gristle. Add Honey Rub to taste and stir in additional Diva Q sauce. Serve the pulled pork on buns with slaw.

Sweet Smoke Q World-Famous Pink Drink

⅓ cup good-quality fresh lemonade

2 oz vodka

2 tbsp cranberry juice

Ice

1 lime wedge

MAKES: 1 serving • **PREP:** 3 minutes

This tangy cocktail is the invention of pitmaster Jim Elser from Winter Haven, FL. Jim and his Sweet Smoke Q team won the World Barbecue Championship in 2014, and he pours his World-Famous Pink Drink at every barbecue competition. You can pair Jim's tipple with all kinds of barbecue, but it's especially good with a pulled pork sandwich drizzled with sweet sauce.

1. Combine the lemonade, vodka and cranberry juice in a cocktail shaker. Add the ice and shake vigorously. **2.** Strain into a glass (over additional ice, if you like) and garnish with the lime wedge.

Peach Nectar Pulled Pork

MAKES 20 to 30 servings • **PREP** 45 minutes • **CHILL** 4 hours • **COOK** 8 to 10 hours • **REST** 2 hours

Friends in Georgia have taught me that injecting peach nectar into a pork butt makes it a thing of beauty. This is my go-to recipe for pulled pork. It makes a big batch, but freezes well.

2 bone-in pork butts (each 10 to 12 lb)
Hickory wood chips
Oak wood chips

Injection
2 cups peach nectar
½ cup packed light brown sugar
¼ cup kosher salt
2 tsp Worcestershire sauce
1 tsp MSG (optional)
1 tsp mustard powder

Rub
Kansas City Rub (page 25; double the recipe)

Spritz
2 cups apple juice

Wrap
1½ cups apple juice
1 cup packed light brown sugar
½ cup hot sauce

Sauce
Kansas City Sweet BBQ Sauce (page 32; double the recipe)

To Serve
Additional Kansas City Sweet BBQ Sauce
Buns and slaw

Q SAVVY

Pulled pork frozen in 2- and 3-pound portions are perfect for family meals during the week. Drizzling with some apple juice before freezing helps keep the meat moist.

1. Trim the tops of the pork butts of excess fat, leaving the bottom fat caps intact. Place each pork butt in a 2-gallon resealable freezer bag. **2.** Whisk together all the injection ingredients in a medium bowl until the sugar and salt have dissolved. Fill the injector with the mixture. **3.** Inject half of the injection into each pork butt, injecting the butts every ½ inch. **4.** Rub each pork butt in its bag generously with the Kansas City rub. Seal the bags and refrigerate the pork butts for 4 hours. **5.** Pour the apple juice into a spray bottle. **6.** Prepare your smoker or grill for indirect cooking and preheat it to 225°F to 250°F. Add a small handful each of hickory and oak chips, following the instructions on page 9 for your type of smoker or grill. **7.** When the wood chips start to smoke, place the pork butts on the cool side of the grill. **8.** Smoke the pork butts until the internal temperature of each reaches 165°F to 170°F and they are a deep reddish mahogany, 6 to 7 hours. Replenish the wood chips by adding a handful of each every hour while the pork butts smoke. **9.** Check the pork butts every 30 minutes. If their surfaces seem dry, spritz them so they are moist but not dripping. **10.** After 6 or 7 hours, place each pork butt in a disposable aluminum pan. (Leave the grill on.) **11.** Sprinkle each pork butt with half of the apple juice, half of the brown sugar and half of the hot sauce. Cover each pan with heavy-duty foil, sealing it tightly. **12.** Return the pans to the cool side of the grill and grill until the internal temperature of each pork butt reaches 200°F and the bone can be pulled out easily, 2 to 3 hours. Remove the pans from the grill. **13.** Strain the pan juices through a fine-mesh sieve. Add the strained juices to the Kansas City sauce and whisk thoroughly. Glaze each pork butt with the sauce. **14.** Cover the pans with plastic wrap and a double layer of foil. Place the pans in a cooler or a very large plastic container and cover them with towels. Let the pork butts rest for 2 hours. **15.** To serve, pull the pork butts into large chunks, discarding any fat and gristle. Mix with additional barbecue sauce and serve on buns with slaw.

Q SAVVY

For a different take on nachos, swap
out the pulled pork for pulled
Roadside Chicken (page 156).

Pulled Pork Nachos

MAKES: 8 to 10 servings • **PREP:** 20 minutes • **COOK:** 10 to 20 minutes

My kids are nacho addicts, and this is their favorite snack. Since we always have pulled pork in the freezer (see page 77), this recipe is an easy fix. It's the perfect party/football/making-people-happy snack. We sometimes have a nacho bar party at which we set out bowls of ingredients and let everyone make their own nachos in small cast iron pans.

1 large bag corn tortilla chips

2 cups warm Peach Nectar Pulled Pork (page 77) or World Championship–Winning Pulled Pork (page 75)

½ cup Diva Q Competition Sauce (page 33)

2 cups shredded cold-smoked cheddar or pepper Jack (page 18)

½ cup pitted, sliced black or green olives

1 small red onion, finely chopped

1 cup chopped tomatoes

1 cup seeded and chopped sweet peppers

1 cup sliced fresh or drained, pickled jalapeños (or to taste)

Sour cream

Fresh Pineapple Salsa (page 140)

1. Prepare your grill for direct cooking and preheat it to medium-high (375°F to 450°F). **2.** Spread one-third of the tortilla chips over the bottom of a disposable aluminum pan. **3.** Top the tortilla chips with one-third of the pulled pork, one-third of the sauce, one-third of the shredded cheese, one-third of the olives and one-third of the onion. Repeat these layers twice. **4.** Place the pan on the grill and grill until the cheese is thoroughly melted, 10 to 20 minutes. **5.** Remove the pan from the grill and top the nachos with tomatoes, sweet peppers and jalapeños. Serve with sour cream and salsa on the side.

Krunkarita

MAKES: 4 servings • **PREP:** 15 minutes • **COOK:** 2 to 3 minutes

Andy Allen and Randy Hill, of the Southern Krunk BBQ Society in Arkansas, created this recipe. It's the best-ever margarita and a natural with the nachos. The only tweak I've made is to add grilled limes.

1 cup granulated sugar

1 cup water

1 cup freshly squeezed lemon juice

8 oz Don Julio Blanco or your favorite tequila

4 oz Cointreau

8 limes, divided

½ cup kosher salt

Ice

1. Mix together the sugar and water in a medium saucepan. Bring to a boil, stirring to dissolve the sugar. Remove the saucepan from the heat. Let the syrup cool, then pour into a pitcher and refrigerate until chilled. **2.** Add the lemon juice, tequila and Cointreau to the syrup. Refrigerate until ready to serve. **3.** Prepare your grill for direct cooking and preheat it to medium-high (375°F to 450°F). **4.** Cut 4 of the limes into ¼-inch slices. Grill the lime slices, turning once, until grill marks appear, 2 to 3 minutes. Remove the lime slices from the grill and set aside. **5.** Grate the zest from the remaining limes. Mix together the lime zest and salt in a small bowl. **6.** Rim 4 glasses with a slice of grilled lime, then rim with lime salt. **7.** Shake the tequila mixture with ice in a cocktail shaker. Strain into the glasses and add a squeeze of grilled lime to each.

Pulled Pork
Double-Stuffed Potatoes

MAKES 6 to 8 servings • **PREP** 15 minutes • **COOK** 1³/₄ to 2¹/₄ hours

Because I enter so many competitions throughout the year, I end up with a lot of leftover cooked meat, so have figured out a bunch of easy ways to use it up. Potatoes make the perfect vessels for pulled pork and barbecue sauce. I like cheddar, bacon, chives and chilies with mine, but play around with your own favorite toppings.

Hickory wood chips

8 medium red potatoes, scrubbed

½ cup bacon grease, melted

Kosher salt and finely ground black pepper to taste

1 cup sour cream

1 cup unsalted butter, melted

2 cups Peach Nectar Pulled Pork (page 77)

Kansas City Sweet BBQ Sauce to taste (page 32)

1 cup shredded Jack cheddar

8 slices bacon, cooked and crumbled

2 tbsp finely chopped fresh chives

Seeded and finely chopped chilies to taste (optional)

Additional sour cream and Kansas City Sweet BBQ Sauce

1. Prepare your grill for indirect cooking and preheat it to 250°F. Add a handful of hickory chips, following the instructions on page 9 for your type of smoker or grill. 2. Pierce each potato a couple of times with a fork. Combine the potatoes, bacon grease, and salt and pepper to taste in a large bowl and toss to coat well. 3. When the chips start to smoke, place the potatoes on the cool side of the grill. Smoke the potatoes until they are tender, 1½ to 2 hours. Replenish the wood chips by adding another handful every 30 minutes. 4. Remove the potatoes from the grill. (Leave the grill on.) Carefully slice each potato in half lengthwise. Scoop the potato flesh into a medium bowl, reserving the potato skins. 5. Add the sour cream, butter, and salt and pepper to taste to the potato flesh and mash well. Scoop the potato mixture back into the potato skins. 6. Combine the pulled pork with enough sauce to moisten it. Top each potato half with pulled pork, then with cheddar. Return the potato halves to the cool side of the grill and grill until the cheese has melted, 10 to 15 minutes. 7. Serve the stuffed potatoes topped with bacon, chives, chilies, and additional sour cream and sauce.

> ## Q SAVVY
> *Use large russet potatoes and more pulled pork to turn these into a substantial main course.*

Tomahawk Pork Chops with Mango Glaze

MAKES: 4 servings • **PREP:** 20 minutes • **BRINE:** 4 hours • **COOK:** 30 to 40 minutes

Huge beef steaks, known as tomahawk steaks, have been popping up in butcher shops over the last few years. I love the pork version, too. These are great for a dinner party (see the sidebar for a neat way to serve them), and the mango glaze adds a touch of the exotic.

Brine

3 cups water
¼ cup good-quality kosher salt
¼ cup packed light brown sugar
½ tsp ground ginger
½ tsp ground allspice
½ tsp finely ground black pepper

Chops

4 bone-in, rib-cut pork chops (1½ inches thick)
Kosher salt and finely ground black pepper to taste

Glaze

1 large mango, peeled, pitted and sliced
1 jalapeño, seeded and minced
Half small sweet white onion, minced
2 tbsp packed light brown sugar
2 tbsp apple cider vinegar
½ tsp minced fresh ginger
½ tsp fresh thyme leaves
½ tsp cinnamon

1. Whisk together all the brine ingredients in a plastic container large enough to hold the pork chops. Whisk until the salt and sugar have dissolved. Place the pork chops in the brine and refrigerate for 4 hours. **2.** Mix together all the glaze ingredients in a medium saucepan. Simmer, stirring occasionally, until the mango has softened, 15 to 20 minutes. Set aside to cool. **3.** Remove the chops from the brine, discarding the brine. Pat the chops dry on paper towels and season with salt and pepper to taste. **4.** Prepare your grill for indirect cooking and preheat it to medium-high (375°F to 450°F). **5.** Place the chops on the hot side of the grill and grill until lightly crusted, 5 to 6 minutes per side. **6.** Glaze the chops on both sides with the mango mixture and move them to the cool side of the grill. Grill, turning and brushing with the glaze once, until the internal temperature reaches 140°F, 12 to 15 minutes. **7.** Remove the chops from the grill, tent loosely with foil and let rest for 5 minutes. Serve with any remaining glaze.

Peachy Jack

7 oz peach cider
1 oz Jack Daniel's Whiskey
Ice
1 peach slice
1 cocktail stick

MAKES: 1 serving • **PREP:** 5 minutes

This refreshing tipple is a must with the mango-glazed pork chops.

1. Combine the cider and whiskey in a cocktail shaker. Add ice and shake vigorously. Strain into a chilled glass. **2.** Skewer the peach slice on a cocktail stick, add to the drink and serve.

Q SAVVY

For a fun presentation, cut a small slice off the meaty end of the pork chops and serve them standing up.

Rosemary-Garlic Slathered Chops

MAKES 8 servings • **PREP** 15 minutes • **BRINE** 3 hours • **COOK** 15 to 20 minutes

Thick pork chops grilled right can be just as satisfying as the best-ever steak. The secret to keeping them juicy on the grill is a simple savory brine. Here, rosemary and pepper in the brine give the chops big flavor. I get a lot of my pork from the Hill family at Willowgrove Hill Farms, Mitchell, ON. Great people; great pork.

8 center-cut boneless pork chops, about 1 inch thick

Rosemary-Pepper Brine

16 cups water

½ cup kosher salt

¼ cup packed light brown sugar

2 tbsp whole black peppercorns

2 sprigs fresh rosemary, leaves picked and coarsely chopped

Rosemary-Garlic Slather

¼ cup Dijon mustard

¼ cup extra virgin olive oil

2 tbsp minced garlic

1 tsp kosher salt

½ tsp finely ground black pepper

1 small bunch fresh rosemary, leaves picked and finely chopped

1. In a large plastic container, whisk together all the brine ingredients until the salt and sugar have dissolved. Add the chops to the brine and refrigerate for 3 hours. **2.** Mix together all the slather ingredients in a small bowl. Remove the chops from the brine and pat them dry. Generously spread the slather all over both sides of the chops. **3.** Prepare your grill for direct cooking and preheat it to high (450°F). **4.** Grill the chops, turning once, until the internal temperature reaches 140°F, 15 to 20 minutes. **5.** Remove the chops from the grill, tent loosely with foil and let rest for 5 minutes before serving.

Q SAVVY

The Rosemary-Garlic Slather is also fantastic smeared on whole cuts of pork or prime rib.

Grilled Pork Cheeks with Apricot Glaze

MAKES: 4 servings • **PREP:** 15 minutes • **COOK:** 40 to 60 minutes

People need to eat more pork cheeks. Period. Tender and flavorful, pork cheeks just need a little trimming (see method). A short braise after grilling breaks down the fibers and makes the pork cheeks tender but still with a bit of chew. I love apricots in any form—fresh, dried, or in a jelly or glaze—and they pair perfectly with any type of pork.

1 medium white sweet onion, cut in half, leaving root end intact

3 lb pork cheeks, trimmed

Kosher salt and finely ground black pepper to taste

Canola oil for oiling

1 cup apple juice

Glaze

1 cup apricot preserves

2 tbsp packed light brown sugar

2 tbsp Dijon mustard

½ tsp ground ginger

1. Prepare your grill for direct cooking and preheat it to medium-high (375°F to 450°F). 2. Grill the onion, turning often, until lightly charred, 6 to 7 minutes. Remove the onion from the grill. When cool enough to handle, slice the onion, discarding the root end. Set the sliced onion aside. 3. With a small, sharp knife, trim the silvery membrane from the pork cheeks. Season the pork cheeks with salt and pepper to taste. 4. Oil the grill grates, then grill the pork cheeks until lightly charred and seared, 2 to 3 minutes on each side. 5. Remove the pork cheeks to a large cast iron skillet. Place the skillet on the grill. Add the apple juice and grilled onion to the skillet, cover with foil and braise until the pork cheeks are tender and the internal temperature reaches 155°F to 160°F, 20 to 30 minutes. 6. Meanwhile, mix together all the glaze ingredients in a medium bowl. 7. Remove the skillet from the grill. Remove the pork cheeks from the skillet and place them directly on the grill. 8. Reserving the onion, pour the cooking juices from the skillet into the bowl of glaze. Brush the glaze over both sides of the pork cheeks. Grill the pork cheeks, turning once, until the glaze has caramelized, 10 to 20 minutes. 9. Remove the pork cheeks from the grill and serve with the grilled onion.

Q SAVVY

The cheeks—tender and flavorful from the fats that run through them—are one of the most delicious yet underutilized cuts of meat on a pig. Ask your butcher to order them for you.

Pork Steaks with Cherry-Chipotle Glaze

MAKES: 6 servings • **PREP:** 10 minutes • **COOK:** about 25 minutes

I didn't eat my first pork steak until a few years ago. I was at a barbecue competition and one of the teams brought them to a potluck. Since then, this recipe has become a regular weeknight meal for our family. It's economical, and the cherry-chipotle glaze makes the steaks darn tasty.

6 bone-in pork steaks (1 inch thick)
Kansas City Rub (page 25)
Cherry-Chipotle BBQ Sauce (page 37)

1. Prepare your grill for indirect cooking and preheat it to medium-high (375°F to 450°F). **2.** Generously season the pork steaks on both sides with the rub. Grill the pork steaks on the hot side of the grill, turning once, until lightly charred, 12 to 16 minutes. **3.** Glaze the steaks generously on both sides with the sauce. Grill the steaks on the cool side of the grill, turning once, until the internal temperature reaches 140°F, about 10 minutes. **4.** Remove the steaks from the grill, tent loosely with foil and let rest for 5 minutes before serving.

Q SAVVY

For fall-off-the-bone-tender pork steaks, after charring them, place the steaks in a disposable aluminum pan. Add 2 cups apple juice and cover the pan with foil. Place the pan on the cool side of the grill and grill for 1½ hours. Remove the steaks from the pan, return them directly to the grill and glaze as described in the recipe.

Double-Smoked Maple-Mustard Easter Ham

MAKES: 16 servings • **PREP:** 15 minutes • **COOK:** 2³/₄ hours

We always have a crowd at our house for Easter. Friends pop by, the bunny does his thing and I get to make my favorite ham, glazed with the sweet-savory notes of maple and mustard. This is a great recipe for people who like to putter by the grill. Keep glazing the ham until you're happy with the result. If you enjoy a super-sweet ham, double up on the glaze and baste away until you reach your ham-happiness level.

Hickory, oak or maple wood chips
8 lb smoked spiral-cut, bone-in ham
2 cups apple juice

Glaze
½ cup packed dark brown sugar
½ cup amber maple syrup
¼ cup Dijon mustard
½ tsp ground allspice
½ tsp finely ground black pepper

1. Prepare your smoker or grill for indirect cooking and preheat it to 250°F. Add a handful of wood chips, following the instructions on page 9 for your type of smoker or grill. **2.** Place the ham in a large disposable aluminum pan. Pour the apple juice into a spray bottle. Spritz the ham with apple juice. **3.** When the wood chips start to smoke, place the pan of ham on the cool side of the grill. Smoke the ham for 2 hours, spritzing it with apple juice every 15 minutes. Replenish the wood chips by adding another handful every 30 minutes while the ham smokes. **4.** Meanwhile, mix together all the glaze ingredients in a medium bowl. **5.** Increase the temperature of the grill to 300°F. Grill the ham, basting it with glaze every 15 minutes and making sure to get the glaze in between the ham's slices, until the baste has caramelized and the internal temperature reaches 140°F, about 45 minutes. **6.** Remove the ham from the grill, tent loosely with foil and let rest for 15 minutes before slicing. Serve with the accumulated pan juices.

Q SAVVY

Be sure to save the ham bone and add it to the pot when you make Smoked Pork Hock Bean Soup (page 105).

Lip-Smacking Dry (or Wet) Ribs

MAKES: 4 to 6 servings • **PREP:** 30 minutes • **MARINATE:** 30 minutes • **COOK:** 4 to 5 hours

I get asked for advice on how to cook ribs more than any other topic. And no wonder. Ribs are easy to love. There's something primal about a slab of ribs kissed with smoke, rubbed with spices and (sometimes) slathered with sauce. Make sure you buy good-quality ribs that are big and meaty. Depending on the weight of the ribs, the cooking time can vary from 4 to 6 hours. If you opt for wet ribs, experiment with different ingredients, such as preserves or pepper jellies, in the foil wrap.

2 racks St. Louis–style pork ribs (see sidebar)
2 tbsp yellow mustard
Hickory wood chips

For Dry Ribs
¾ cup Memphis Rib Rub (page 24)

For Wet Ribs
¾ cup Kansas City Rub (page 25)
½ cup apple juice
1 cup packed light brown sugar
¼ cup hot sauce

Spritz
1 cup apple juice

To Finish
1½ cups Kansas City Sweet BBQ Sauce (page 32), plus additional sauce to serve

1. Prepare your grill for indirect cooking and preheat it to 225°F to 250°F. 2. Rinse the ribs under cool, running water and pat dry. Remove the membrane from the bony side of the ribs (see sidebar, page 92). 3. Coat the ribs thinly on both sides with mustard. Rub the ribs on both sides with 3 to 4 tbsp of the rub of your choice. Set the ribs aside for 30 minutes to allow the rub to penetrate. 4. Add a handful of hickory chips, following the instructions on page 9 for your type of smoker or grill. When the chips start to smoke, place the ribs on the cool side of the grill, meat side up. Smoke the ribs for 1 hour. 5. After 1 hour, pour the apple juice into a spray bottle and spritz the ribs. Add another handful of wood chips to the grill. Smoke the ribs for 1 hour, then spritz again and replenish the wood chips. 6. For dry ribs, smoke for an additional 2 hours, spritzing regularly with apple juice. Serve without sauce. (The remaining steps are for wet ribs only.) 7. For wet ribs, remove the ribs from the grill after the first 3 hours of cooking. 8. Lay out a large piece of foil 2½ times the length of the racks of ribs. Fold the foil in half. Place one rack of ribs on the foil meat side down. Pour half the apple juice overtop, then sprinkle with half of the sugar and half of the hot sauce. Wrap the ribs in the foil, sealing the edges tightly to ensure the juices stay in. 9. Repeat with the second rack of ribs and the remaining apple juice, sugar and hot sauce. 10. Return the wrapped ribs to the cool side of the grill, making sure they are bone side down. Grill until the ribs are tender, 45 minutes to 1 hour. The meat will start to crack and split when the ribs are ready. If they're not tender to your liking, keep checking every 15 minutes.

11. Carefully unwrap the ribs and place them on a rimmed baking sheet, discarding the juices in the foil. **12.** Prepare the grill for direct cooking and increase the temperature to 300°F. Brush the ribs on both sides with barbecue sauce. Grill the ribs, watching them closely and rotating and flipping the racks once, until the sauce is set and the sugars have caramelized, 5 to 10 minutes. **13.** Remove the ribs from the grill, tent loosely with foil and let them rest for 10 minutes. **14.** Turn the ribs meat side down and slice cleanly between the bones. Serve with additional barbecue sauce on the side.

Q SAVVY

St. Louis–style pork ribs are my favorite cut for competitions. They're side ribs that have had the brisket and sternum bones trimmed off to create a neat, rectangular rack of ribs.

Make sure to remove the membrane from the bony side of a slab of ribs to allow the flavors of a rub to be absorbed. To remove the membrane, insert the tip of your finger under the membrane in the center of the rack and work a section loose. Grasp the loosened membrane with a piece of paper towel and peel it off.

Nibble-Me-This Pork Tenderloin with Thai Peanut Sauce

MAKES: 6 servings • **PREP:** 15 minutes • **MARINATE:** 4 to 6 hours • **COOK:** about 25 minutes

My talented friend Chris Grove from Knoxville, TN, who loves to grill almost as much as I do, came up with this recipe for tenderloin with Thai peanut sauce. It's wicked good and packs a punch of flavor. Make it, love it and be sure to visit Chris's website: nibblemethis.com.

2 pork tenderloins, silver skin trimmed

Marinade

⅓ cup peanut oil
¼ cup finely chopped fresh cilantro
1 tbsp freshly squeezed lime juice
2 tsp fish sauce
1 tsp toasted sesame oil
1 tsp Sriracha sauce
2 cloves garlic, smashed
½ tsp light brown sugar
½ tsp ground ginger

Peanut Sauce

⅓ cup teriyaki sauce
¼ cup smooth peanut butter
1 tbsp rice wine vinegar
½ tsp dehydrated sweet red pepper flakes
¼ tsp ground ginger

1. Put the tenderloins in a large, resealable freezer bag. 2. Put all the marinade ingredients in a food processor and process for 30 seconds. 3. Pour the marinade into the bag, making sure the tenderloins are completely coated. Seal the bag and refrigerate for 4 to 6 hours. 4. Put all the peanut sauce ingredients in a food processor and process for 30 seconds until well blended. Refrigerate until needed. (Peanut sauce can be made ahead.) 5. When ready to cook, prepare your grill for direct cooking and preheat it to 375°F. 6. Remove the tenderloins from the marinade. Grill the tenderloins, rotating them every 5 minutes, until the thickest parts reach an internal temperature of 140°F, about 20 minutes. 7. Remove the tenderloins from the grill, tent loosely with foil and let rest for 5 minutes before serving. 8. While the tenderloins are resting, heat the peanut sauce in a small saucepan over medium-low heat for 3 to 5 minutes. 9. Cut the tenderloins into ¼-inch slices. Drizzle with peanut sauce and serve with more sauce on the side for dipping.

Q SAVVY

Versatile pork tenderloin tapers at one end. For even cooking, arrange the tenderloins on your grill with the thicker ends toward your grill's hot spots.

Perfectly Easy Porchetta

MAKES 12 to 16 servings • **PREP** 45 minutes • **COOK** about 5½ hours

Good grief, I crave porchetta! It's sinfully decadent and good served hot or cold the next day in sandwiches. There are so many versions of porchetta. I like to use fennel in mine, but you can substitute any hardy greens, such as kale or mustard greens, or just leave it out altogether.

¼ cup unsalted butter

1 medium bulb fennel, thinly sliced

3 stalks celery, thinly sliced

2 small white sweet onions, thinly sliced

6 to 7 lb skin-on pork belly (in one piece)

Kosher salt and finely ground black pepper to taste

12 cloves garlic, minced

1 bunch fresh rosemary, leaves picked and finely chopped

1 bunch fresh flat-leaf parsley, leaves picked and finely chopped

¼ cup extra virgin olive oil

2 lemons, zested and juiced

2 tbsp fennel seeds

2 tbsp Dijon mustard

1 tbsp ground sage

Hickory wood chips

1. Melt the butter in a medium saucepan over medium heat. Sauté the fennel, celery and onions until softened but not browned. Remove the saucepan from the heat and set aside to cool to room temperature. **2.** Place the pork belly, skin side down, on a cutting board. Generously season the meat side of the belly with salt and pepper. **3.** In a food processor, combine the garlic, rosemary, parsley, oil, lemon zest, lemon juice, fennel seeds, mustard and sage. Pulse just enough to make a paste. **4.** Spread three-quarters of the garlic mixture on the meat side of the pork belly. Top with the fennel mixture. Roll the pork belly up tightly and tie in 2 or 3 places with butcher twine. **5.** With a sharp knife, score the skin of the pork belly in between the twine. Rub the remaining garlic mixture into the score marks on the skin. Season the pork belly all over with salt and pepper. **6.** Prepare your smoker or grill for indirect cooking and preheat it to 225°F. Add a handful of hickory chips, following the instructions on page 9 for your type of smoker or grill. **7.** When the chips start to smoke, place the pork belly on the cool side of the grill. Smoke the pork belly for 4 hours, adding another handful of wood chips every hour. **8.** Increase the temperature of the grill to 375°F. Smoke the pork belly until the internal temperature reaches 155°F to 160°F, about 1½ hours. Replenish the wood chips by adding another handful halfway through the cooking time. **9.** Remove the porchetta from the grill, tent loosely with foil and let rest for at least 15 minutes before slicing.

East-Meets-West Stuffed Pork Loin

MAKES: 6 servings • **PREP:** 45 minutes • **MARINATE:** overnight • **COOK:** about 2 hours

This was one of the first recipes I wrote after becoming an OCB (obsessive-compulsive barbecuer). Fast-forward many years and my family still asks for this recipe. It works well for a dinner party or simple Sunday supper. For best results, use cornbread that is a couple of days old.

3 lb boneless, butterflied pork loin

Marinade
½ cup packed light brown sugar
¼ cup red wine vinegar
¼ cup ketchup
¼ cup hoisin sauce
2 tbsp low-sodium soy sauce
2 tbsp minced garlic
1 tsp five-spice powder
1 tsp ground ginger
½ tsp table salt
½ tsp finely ground black pepper

Stuffing
2 tbsp unsalted butter
1 medium white sweet onion, finely chopped
4 cups crumbled Buttery Cornbread (page 235)
2 tbsp dried chives
1 tsp ground sage
½ cup chicken stock
1 tsp kosher salt
½ tsp finely ground black pepper

Glaze
½ cup low-sodium soy sauce
¼ cup hoisin sauce
2 tsp toasted sesame oil
1 tsp rice wine vinegar

1. Place the pork loin in a large resealable freezer bag. Mix together all the marinade ingredients in a medium bowl. Add the marinade to the bag, turning to coat the pork. Seal the bag and refrigerate overnight. **2.** The next day, remove the pork loin from the marinade, discarding the remaining marinade. Set the pork aside. **3.** For the stuffing, melt the butter in a large skillet over medium heat. Sauté the onion until softened but not browned. Stir in the cornbread, chives and sage. **4.** Remove the skillet from the heat. Add the chicken stock, salt and pepper. Let cool to room temperature. **5.** Cover a large cutting board with plastic wrap. Lay the pork loin, cut side up, on the plastic wrap. Spread the cornbread stuffing over the pork loin to cover the top side completely. Using the plastic wrap to lift it, roll up the pork loin tightly, jelly roll style. Tie at 1-inch intervals with butcher twine. **6.** Prepare your grill for indirect cooking and preheat it to 250°F. **7.** Place the pork loin on the cool side of the grill and grill until the internal temperature reaches 135°F, 1½ to 2 hours. **8.** Meanwhile mix together all the glaze ingredients in a small bowl. **9.** Brush the glaze all over the pork loin and continue grilling until the internal temperature reaches 140°F, 15 to 20 minutes. **10.** Remove the pork loin from the grill, tent loosely with foil and let rest for 15 minutes before slicing.

Q SAVVY

For smoky pork, add a handful of wood chips every 30 minutes while the pork cooks. Fruit woods (cherry, apple) and lighter woods (pecan) pair well with pork.

Filipino-Style Stuffed Pork Belly

MAKES: 16 servings • **PREP:** 30 minutes • **COOK:** 7 to 8 hours

Traditional Filipino *cebu lechon* involves cooking a whole stuffed pig on a massive rotisserie over a charcoal fire until its skin turns to glistening crackling. Delicious but far from feasible for most people. So I came up with a simpler recipe that still captures the same incredible flavor. The skin on this pork is insanely good—my family actually fights over the crackling.

8 lb skin-on pork belly (in one piece)

5 cloves garlic, smashed

¼ cup dried chives

¼ cup kosher salt

3 tbsp finely ground black pepper

5 bay leaves, crushed

10 stalks lemongrass, bruised (see sidebar)

1 bunch green onions, trimmed

1 bunch garlic chives

2 cups good-quality soy sauce, such as China Lily

Hickory wood chips

1. Lay the pork belly, skin side down, on a cutting board.
2. Mix together the garlic, dried chives, salt, pepper and bay leaves in a small bowl. Rub the garlic mixture all over the meat side of the pork belly. Arrange the lemongrass, green onions and garlic chives lengthwise down the center of the pork belly. 3. Bring the sides of the pork belly together and tie tightly with butcher twine to make a neat cylinder. Brush the skin with some of the soy sauce. 4. Prepare your smoker or grill for indirect cooking and preheat it to 250°F. Add a handful of hickory chips, following the instructions on page 9 for your type of smoker or grill. 5. When the chips start to smoke, place the pork belly on the cool side of the grill. Smoke the pork belly, basting every 30 minutes with more soy sauce, until the internal temperature of the pork reaches 155°F to 160°F and the skin is crispy, 7 to 8 hours. Replenish the wood chips by adding two handfuls every hour while the pork belly smokes. 6. Remove the pork belly from the grill, tent loosely with foil and let rest for 15 minutes before slicing thinly.

Q SAVVY

Bruising the lemongrass stalks helps release their aromatic flavoring. Use the handle of a heavy chef's knife or the base of a small saucepan to pound the lemongrass.

Belly, Jelly and Biscuits

MAKES: 8 servings • **PREP:** 15 minutes • **MARINATE:** overnight • **COOK:** about 2¼ hours

I love a good biscuit, and combining one with pork belly and a pepper jelly makes my mouth water and transports me to the Deep South. This way of cooking with pork belly comes from chef Michael Olson, a professor at Ontario's Niagara College, and is worth every minute of prep. The result is an extremely crunchy exterior, almost like *chicharrón*, the Latino pork crackling snack.

2½ lb skin-on pork belly (in one piece)

1 tbsp table salt

1 tsp baking powder

Cherry wood chips

16 Best-Ever Buttermilk Biscuits, split (page 234)

1 jar (12 oz/355 mL) Texas Pepper Jelly Cherry Habanero Jelly or your favorite pepper jelly

1. Using a sharp knife, score the skin side of the pork belly at ¼-inch intervals, cutting just into the fat but not through the meat. 2. Stir together the salt and baking powder in a small bowl. Rub the mixture into the scored skin of the pork belly. 3. Place the belly, skin side up, in a shallow nonmetallic dish and refrigerate overnight. 4. The next day, prepare your smoker or grill for indirect cooking and preheat it to 250°F. Add a handful of cherry chips, following the instructions on page 9 for your type of smoker or grill. 5. When the chips start to smoke, place the pork belly, skin side up, on a wire rack over a large disposable aluminum pan. Place the pan on the cool side of the grill. 6. Smoke the pork belly for 2 hours. Replenish the wood chips by adding another handful every 30 minutes while the pork belly smokes.

7. Remove the pan from the grill, cover the pork belly loosely with foil and let rest for 30 minutes. Increase the temperature of the grill to 450°F to 500°F. 8. Place the pork belly, skin side down, directly on the grill grates on the cool side of the grill. Smoke until the internal temperature reaches 155°F to 160°F and the skin is golden and has puffed up, 8 to 10 minutes. 9. Remove the pork belly from the grill. Flip so the pork belly is skin side up, cover loosely with foil and let rest for 15 minutes. Slice the pork belly thinly and serve in the biscuits with pepper jelly.

Smoked Sausage Biscuits and Gravy

MAKES: 6 servings • **PREP:** 20 minutes • **COOK:** about 1 hour

Who can resist a biscuit? Fluffy buttermilk biscuits and rich sausage gravy are over-the-top indulgent, and I am not even going to try to pretend this is healthy, but it's worth every calorie. You could just fry up the sausage and crumble it in the gravy, but a little hickory smoke makes all the difference.

Hickory wood chips

1 lb good-quality sausage meat, such as Bob Evans Pork Sausage

2 tbsp all-purpose flour

2 tbsp unsalted butter, softened

2 cups milk

Kosher salt and finely ground black pepper to taste

6 hot Best-Ever Buttermilk Biscuits (page 234)

1. Prepare your smoker or grill for indirect cooking and preheat it to 275°F. Add a handful of hickory chips, following the instructions on page 9 for your type of smoker or grill. 2. Unwrap the sausage meat but leave it in a sausage shape. When the chips start to smoke, place the sausage on the cool side of the grill. Smoke until the internal temperature reaches 160°F, 45 to 60 minutes. Replenish the wood chips by adding another handful halfway through the cooking time. 3. Remove the sausage from the grill. Crumble the sausage meat into a large bowl. Set aside. 4. Whisk together the flour and butter in a large saucepan over medium heat. Cook, stirring often, until pale golden, 5 to 10 minutes. 5. Whisk in the milk until smooth. Cook, whisking constantly, until the sauce is bubbly and smooth. 6. Stir in the sausage meat and bring to a boil. Season the gravy lightly with salt and generously with pepper. Serve over piping hot biscuits.

Q SAVVY

This is a perfect, soul-satisfying breakfast for a crowd. Just don't tell your cardiologist.

Orange-Ginger Pork Kebabs

MAKES: 4 servings • **PREP:** 20 minutes • **COOK:** 20 minutes

Put anything on a stick and the fun factor goes way up. Orange and ginger are a great combo for pork, and the marmalade here turns the kebabs sticky and yummy as you grill them. This recipe also makes a great appetizer if you thread individual cubes of pork onto smaller, appetizer-size skewers.

1½ lb boneless pork loin, cut into 1½-inch chunks

4 metal skewers

Kosher salt and finely ground black pepper to taste

3 oranges, cut into ¼-inch slices

Baste

1 cup orange marmalade

½ cup orange juice with pulp

¼ cup grated fresh ginger

2 tbsp canola oil

1 tbsp dried chives

1 tsp granulated onion (see page 25)

1 tsp minced garlic

1. Thread the pork chunks onto the skewers. Season the pork with salt and pepper to taste. **2.** Whisk together all the baste ingredients in a small bowl. **3.** Prepare your grill for direct cooking and preheat it to medium-high (375°F to 450°F). Oil the grill grates. **4.** Grill the pork kebabs, basting with the marmalade mixture every 5 minutes and turning often, until the internal temperature of the pork reaches 140°F, about 20 minutes. **5.** When the kebabs have been grilling for about 12 minutes, add the orange slices to the grill. Cook the orange slices, turning once, until well marked with grill marks, 6 to 8 minutes. Serve the kebabs with the grilled orange slices.

Q SAVVY

Using metal skewers for kebabs eliminates the need to soak bamboo skewers before threading on the meat. The metal also heats up and cooks the meat more quickly.

Smoked Pork Hock Bean Soup

MAKES: 12 servings • **PREP:** 30 minutes • **COOK:** 5 to 7 hours

My Grandma P never let anything go to waste and always used every scrap of pork she had, so I ate pork hock bean soup often when I was a kid. Now that I'm a grown-up, I find smoke adds another layer of flavor to the soup. This is a dish best served on a chilly fall or winter day with crusty bread and a glass of wine. Consider it a hug in a bowl.

3 fresh pork hocks (each about 1½ lb)

Kansas City Rub (page 25)

Hickory wood chips

2 tbsp canola oil

2 small sweet onions, finely chopped

8 cups chicken stock

1 lb white navy beans, rinsed, picked over, soaked overnight and drained

4 carrots, peeled and chopped

2 cups seeded and chopped roasted red and orange sweet peppers

¼ cup dried chives

2 tbsp minced garlic

2 bay leaves

Finely ground black pepper to taste

1. Coat the pork hocks all over with the rub. Set aside. **2.** Prepare your smoker or grill for indirect cooking and preheat it to 250°F. Add a handful of hickory chips, following the instructions on page 9 for your type of smoker or grill. **3.** When the chips start to smoke, place the hocks on the cool side of the grill. Smoke the hocks until the meat is tender and can be pulled easily from the bone, 4 to 5 hours. Replenish the hickory chips by adding another handful every hour while the hocks smoke. **4.** Remove the hocks from the grill and set aside. **5.** Heat the oil in a large pot over medium heat. Sauté the onions until softened but not browned. Add the pork hocks, stock, beans, carrots, roasted peppers, chives, garlic and bay leaves to the pot. **6.** Bring to a boil over high heat, then reduce the heat to medium-low and simmer, covered, until the beans are soft, 1 to 2 hours. **7.** If the soup is too thick for your liking, add more stock or water. Season with pepper to taste before serving.

Q SAVVY

Smoked turkey legs, which you can buy from some butcher shops, work well as a substitute for pork hocks in the soup.

Bacon-Wrapped Cherry Turkey Breasts (page 120)

BACON BONANZA

I love bacon and believe it's the key to a truly fulfilled life. From savories to sweets, bacon really does make just about anything taste better. (Be sure to read the safety tips in the sidebar on page 108 before you start grilling.)

Saving Your Bacon on the Grill

The combination of bacon fat and a hot grill can be a recipe for a disastrous grease fire unless you take certain precautions. Read these tips before you get grilling:

- Always have baking soda nearby to suppress any grease fires.
- Never throw water on a grease fire.
- Know where your fire extinguisher is at all times.
- Bacon grease splatters can burn you badly, so wear something with long, tight-fitting sleeves to protect your arms.
- Set an empty aluminum tray under the grill grate to catch bacon grease drippings.
- When you're grilling bacon, never leave the grill unattended.
- Make sure your grill is on level ground. An uneven grill can cause grease to drip into the fire source and cause flare-ups.
- Always wait until the grill is cold to remove any bacon grease drippings from the interior of the grill.
- Start with a clean grill every time. After using a grill for bacon, wait for it to cool down, then wipe the grill grates with paper towels to prevent flare-ups the next time you light the grill.
- Bacon fat can go rancid quickly. Wipe down any splatters of bacon grease on the outside of the grill as soon as they happen.

The Ultimate Bacon and Eggs

MAKES: 6 servings • **PREP:** 15 minutes • **COOK:** 35 to 40 minutes

I was at a trade show a few years back and doing some grilling presentations on Traeger pellet grills (see page 260). There happened to be a Cadbury rep at the show who was giving away samples. We had bacon, we had chocolate, so my friend Marc and I decided to get a little adventurous. This recipe may seem crazy, but the combo of sweet, salt and smoke sure tastes good.

Hickory wood chips
6 Cadbury Creme Eggs, frozen
12 thin slices maple bacon

1. Prepare your grill for indirect grilling and preheat it to 225°F. Add a handful of hickory chips, following the instructions on page 9 for your type of smoker or grill. **2.** Remove the foil from the eggs and wrap each one tightly in 2 slices of bacon, making sure to cover each egg completely. **3.** Place the bacon-wrapped eggs on a wire rack set over a disposable aluminum pan. This will allow air to circulate around the chocolate and the bacon fat to drip down. **4.** Place the pan on the cool side of the grill and smoke the bacon-wrapped eggs for 20 minutes. **5.** Remove the bacon-wrapped eggs from the pan and place them directly on the grill grates on the cool side of the grill. Grill until the bacon is crisp to your liking, 15 to 20 minutes. **6.** Remove the bacon-wrapped eggs from the grill and let cool for 15 minutes before serving.

Q SAVVY

Smoked Bacon-Wrapped Crispy Crunch
Experiment with different types of chocolate bars. The ones that work best are solid or have a peanut butter filling. I particularly like using Crispy Crunch bars. Freeze the bars, wrap them in bacon and grill as for The Ultimate Bacon and Eggs.

Pig Candy

MAKES: about 16 slices • **PREP:** 15 minutes • **COOK:** about 1 hour

A picture of pig candy should appear next to the word "addictive" in the dictionary. It is insanely easy to make, and you can crumble it into almost anything—cookies, icing, ice cream or any other sweet treats that need a hit of bacon.

1 lb thinly sliced bacon

½ cup maple syrup or corn syrup

2 cups packed light brown sugar

3 tbsp chipotle powder

Q SAVVY

Be careful when cooking bacon on the grill, and make sure to read the Saving Your Bacon on the Grill tips on page 108 before you begin.

1. Prepare the grill for indirect cooking and preheat it to medium (300°F to 375°F). **2.** Place the bacon slices in a single layer on a large disposable, perforated aluminum pan. Brush each bacon slice with maple syrup. Sprinkle generously with brown sugar, then chipotle powder. **3.** Place the pan on the cool side of the grill and grill until the bacon has absorbed the brown sugar and is crispy, about 1 hour. **4.** Remove the bacon from the pan and place in a single layer on a wire rack set over a rimmed baking sheet. Set aside at room temperature until the surface of the bacon is dry. **5.** Refrigerate in an airtight container with parchment paper between the layers and use within 1 week.

Grilled Poutine and Bacon

MAKES: 6 servings • **PREP:** 20 minutes • **COOK:** 25 to 30 minutes

Canada's "national dish" gets a grilled twist here. The sensational combination of potato, bacon, cheese curds and St-Hubert gravy is comfort food at its best.

3 lb russet potatoes, scrubbed

2 tbsp canola oil

Kosher salt and finely ground black pepper to taste

6 slices thick-cut bacon

1 can (14 oz/398 mL) St-Hubert Poutine Gravy or 1½ cups home-made chicken gravy

1 cup cheese curds

2 tbsp finely chopped fresh chives

1. Prepare your grill for direct cooking and preheat it to medium-high (375°F to 450°F). **2.** Cut the potatoes into wedges. Put the wedges in a microwave-safe bowl. Cover with plastic wrap and microwave on high until almost tender, about 8 minutes. **3.** Add the oil and salt and pepper to taste to the potatoes and toss well. **4.** Grill the potatoes until crispy and lightly charred, 10 to 12 minutes. **5.** Grill the bacon slices, turning once, until crispy, 8 to 10 minutes. **6.** Meanwhile, bring the poutine gravy to a simmer in a small saucepan over medium heat. **7.** Remove the potatoes and bacon from the grill. Chop the bacon and set aside. **8.** Pile the potato wedges on a platter. Top with the cheese curds and gravy. Sprinkle with bacon and chives.

Bacon-Wrapped Cheddar-Stuffed Double Dogs

MAKES: 6 servings • **PREP:** 30 minutes • **COOK:** about 30 minutes

I'm completely biased, but my kids rock. Our mighty munchkins have traveled to many competitions with us and, for the last couple of years, they have been participating in kids' barbecue contests. I was never so nervous as the first time they participated, but they came third with this recipe, and I had tears in my eyes when I heard their names called. It's my youngest kid Gabe's hands-down favorite recipe.

12 all-beef wieners
12 slices sharp cheddar
24 thin slices bacon
6 hot dog buns, toasted
Ketchup and mustard to serve

1. Prepare your grill for indirect cooking and preheat it to 275°F.
2. Slice the wieners almost in half lengthwise, being careful not to cut all the way through. They should open like a book. 3. Open one of the sliced wieners. Top it with 2 slices of cheddar and another wiener, cut side down. Wrap the cheddar-stuffed wieners tightly with 1½ to 2 slices of bacon. 4. Grill the bacon-wrapped wieners for 15 minutes. Flip them over and grill until the bacon starts to crisp and the cheese has melted, about 15 minutes. You may want to move them to the hot side of the grill for the last few minutes of cooking to crisp up the bacon to your liking. 5. Serve the wieners on toasted hot dog buns with the condiments you like (Ella has ketchup; Gabe prefers mustard and ketchup).

Homemade Citrus Ginger Ale

2 cups water
1 cup granulated sugar
1 cup peeled, thinly sliced fresh ginger
1 lemon, zested and juiced
1 lime, zested and juiced
8½ cups sparkling water or club soda
Crushed ice
1 small bunch fresh mint, leaves
   picked

MAKES: 8 to 10 servings • **PREP:** 15 minutes • **COOK:** 20 minutes

We enjoyed this fantastic alcohol-free beverage at a resort in Mexico alongside simple skewers of grilled chicken and beef, but it goes just as well with my kids' double dogs.

1. Mix together the 2 cups water, the sugar and the ginger in a small saucepan. Bring to a boil, stirring to dissolve the sugar. 2. Reduce the heat and simmer until the ginger has softened completely, about 20 minutes. Remove the saucepan from the heat and let stand for 1 hour. 3. Strain the ginger syrup, discarding the ginger. Refrigerate until chilled. 4. Combine the syrup and the lemon and lime zest and juice in a large pitcher. Add the sparkling water. 5. Pour into glasses over crushed ice and garnish with mint leaves.

Atomic Buffalo Turds

MAKES: 16 ABTs • **PREP:** 30 minutes • **COOK:** 1½ to 2 hours

These bacon-wrapped jalapeño poppers—aka ABTs—are the crack of the barbecue world. I remember the first time I tried one, and I'm a certified addict to this day. I like to fill the jalapeños with a three-cheese mixture, but feel free to tweak the filling and spices to make this recipe your own. The longer you smoke the jalapeños, the more their heat is tempered. If you want super-spicy ABTs, don't remove the membranes and seeds from the jalapeños—just remember to warn your guests.

8 jalapeños, halved lengthwise and seeded

16 thin slices bacon

Filling

1 pkg (8 oz/250 g) cream cheese, softened

½ cup freshly grated Parmesan

½ cup shredded smoked mozzarella

¼ cup freshly grated Romano

Half small white sweet onion, finely chopped

2 tsp hot sauce

1 tsp sweet smoked paprika

1 tsp chipotle powder

½ tsp granulated garlic (see page 25)

1. Mix together all of the filling ingredients in a medium bowl.

2. Fill the jalapeños with the cheese mixture and wrap each in 1 slice of bacon, making sure the bacon covers the filling completely.

3. Prepare your grill for indirect cooking and preheat it to 250°F.

4. Place the ABTs, cut sides up, on the cool side of the grill. Grill until the filling is bubbling out at the edges and the bacon is cooked, 1½ to 2 hours.

Q SAVVY

If you're preparing more than one batch of ABTs or are sensitive to the oils in hot peppers, be sure to wear gloves when handling the jalapeños.

Smoked Brisket Bombs

MAKES: 12 appetizer servings • **PREP:** 30 minutes • **COOK:** 1¹/₂ to 2 hours

Leftover smoked brisket usually isn't a burden, but you can only eat so much sliced brisket or burnt ends. When you have 40 to 50 pounds of brisket in your freezer, like I sometimes do, you need to come up with new and interesting ways to use it up. So these brisket bombs were born. The bacon fat, sauce and smoky flavor combine to make these bites taste out of this world. I serve these as party appetizers, and they always disappear quickly.

2 lb flat from 180 Brisket (page 125), cut into 1½-inch cubes

1 lb thinly sliced bacon

Long wooden toothpicks

Cherry wood chips

1 cup Diva Q Competition Sauce (page 33)

1. Wrap each cube of brisket in a slice of bacon, securing with a toothpick. **2.** Prepare your smoker or grill for indirect cooking and preheat it to 225°F. Add a handful of cherry chips, following the instructions on page 9 for your type of smoker or grill. **3.** When the chips start to smoke, place the brisket bombs on the cool side of the grill. Smoke the brisket bombs for 1 hour. **4.** Flip the brisket bombs over and smoke until the bacon is crisp, 30 minutes to 1 hour. Glaze with the sauce and serve.

Q SAVVY

Put a slice of drained, pickled jalapeño on top of each cube of brisket before wrapping them in bacon for a spiced-up version of Brisket Bombs.

Mulled Jack Daniel's

6 quarts apple juice

1 bottle (26 oz/750 mL) Jack Daniel's Whiskey

¼ cup dried cranberries

2 dried figs

4 pieces candied ginger

3 cinnamon sticks

1 tbsp whole allspice berries

4 whole cloves

2 whole star anise

MAKES: 12 to 18 servings • **PREP:** 10 minutes • **COOK:** 2 to 3 hours

My sister-in-smoke Angie Quaale came up with this recipe one cold winter's night, and I've been enjoying it ever since. Team with the Smoked Brisket Bombs and you've got a holiday party to remember.

1. Mix together all the ingredients in a large pot. Bring just to a simmer over very low heat. Simmer for 2 to 3 hours (do not boil). **2.** Strain through a fine-mesh sieve into a pitcher and serve warm.

Bacon-Wrapped Smoked Stuffed Cherry Peppers

MAKES: 12 stuffed cherry peppers • **PREP:** 30 minutes • **COOK:** 1¹/₂ to 2 hours

Cherry peppers are flavorful but not too spicy, and, filled with cheesy goodness and wrapped in bacon love, they make great appetizers. You can make these as mild or spicy as you like by adjusting the amount of hot sauce.

12 cherry peppers
4 oz herb-and-garlic cream cheese
4 oz soft goat cheese
1 tsp hot sauce
½ tsp sweet smoked paprika
12 slices medium-sliced bacon
Canola oil cooking spray
Cherry wood chips

Q SAVVY

For one heck of a spicy version of this recipe, substitute habaneros for the cherry peppers.

1. With a small, sharp knife, cut out the stem ends of the peppers and carefully scrape out the seeds and membranes from the insides, leaving the peppers whole. **2.** Mix together the cream cheese, goat cheese, hot sauce and paprika in a small bowl. Fill the cavity of each pepper with the cheese mixture. **3.** Wrap each pepper in a slice of bacon, leaving the top of the pepper exposed. **4.** Spray a 12-cup mini cupcake pan with cooking spray. Place a bacon-wrapped pepper, cut side up, in each cavity. **5.** Prepare your smoker or grill for indirect cooking and preheat it to 250°F. Add a handful of cherry chips, following the instructions on page 9 for your type of smoker or grill. **6.** When the chips start to smoke, place the pan of peppers on the cool side of the grill. Smoke until the bacon is crispy and the filling is bubbling, 1½ to 2 hours. Replenish the wood chips by adding another handful every 30 minutes while the peppers smoke.

Bacon-Wrapped Sausage Fatty

MAKES: 8 servings • **PREP:** 20 minutes • **COOK:** 1 ½ to 2 hours

When someone at a barbecue competition asks you if you want to smoke a fatty, we're talking about the sausage version. Use whatever sausage meat you like. Just make sure the fat content isn't too high or your fatty will crumble and fall through the grill grates, and you will be sad.

2 lb good-quality hot (spicy) sausage meat, such as Jimmy Dean Hot Sausage

1 small jalapeño, minced

1 tbsp Canadian Rub (page 26)

1 lb medium-sliced maple bacon

Cherry wood chips

Apple-Beer BBQ Sauce (page 38)

1. Crumble the sausage into a medium bowl. Add the jalapeño and rub and mix well. **2.** Form the sausage mixture into a log shape, about 8 × 4 inches. Wrap the bacon slices tightly around the log, overlapping the slices slightly. **3.** Prepare your smoker or grill for indirect cooking and preheat it to 250°F. Add a handful of cherry chips, following the instructions on page 9 for your type of smoker or grill. **4.** When the chips start to smoke, place the bacon-wrapped sausage fatty on the cool side of the grill. Smoke the fatty until the internal temperature reaches 160°F and the bacon is crisp, 1 ½ to 2 hours. Replenish the cherry chips by adding another handful to the grill every 30 minutes while the fatty smokes. **5.** During the last few minutes of cooking, glaze the fatty with the sauce. **6.** Remove the fatty from the grill, tent loosely with foil and let rest for at least 10 minutes before slicing.

Q SAVVY

When it comes to making a sausage fatty, the options are endless: stuff it with cheese, nix the jalapeños to make it milder or sub in minced ghost peppers for a crazy hot fatty.

Better-Than-Your-Momma's Meatloaf

MAKES: 8 servings • **PREP:** 30 minutes • **CHILL:** overnight • **COOK:** about 2 hours

"Better than your momma's" is quite the statement, but in this case, it's true. This recipe takes meatloaf to a whole new level. Ground chuck and brisket give it great texture, and the cold-smoked cheeses add so much flavor. Add jalapeños and smoke and you have an exceptional meatloaf you'll be proud to serve to anyone. Even your momma.

1 lb ground chuck

1 lb ground beef brisket

1 cup panko bread crumbs

1 medium onion, minced

2 eggs, lightly beaten

2 jalapeños, seeded and minced

2 cloves garlic, minced

Kosher salt and finely ground black pepper to taste

1 cup shredded cold-smoked cheddar (page 18)

1 cup shredded cold-smoked pepper Jack (page 18)

Pecan wood chips

Kansas City Rub (page 25)

1 lb thinly sliced smoked bacon

Kansas City Sweet BBQ Sauce (page 32)

1. Gently mix together the ground chuck and brisket, bread crumbs, onion, eggs, jalapeños, garlic, and salt and pepper to taste in a large bowl. Pack half of the mixture into a 9- × 5-inch loaf pan. **2.** Make a well in the center of the meat mixture in the pan and add the cheeses to the well. Top the cheeses with the remaining meatloaf mixture, packing it tightly. Cover the pan tightly with plastic wrap and refrigerate overnight to set the mixture. **3.** The next day, prepare your smoker or grill for indirect cooking and preheat it to 250°F. Add a handful of pecan chips, following the instructions on page 9 for your type of smoker or grill. **4.** Carefully remove the meatloaf from the pan. Season the meatloaf all over with the rub. Cover the meatloaf with the bacon slices, overlapping the slices slightly and making sure the ends are tucked under. **5.** When the pecan chips are smoking, place the meatloaf on the cool side of the grill. Smoke the meatloaf until the internal temperature reaches 155°F, 1½ to 2 hours. Replenish the wood chips by adding another handful every 30 minutes while the meatloaf smokes. **6.** Brush the meatloaf with the sauce. Smoke the meatloaf until the internal temperature reaches 160°F, about 15 minutes. **7.** Remove the meatloaf from the grill, tent loosely with foil and let rest for 10 minutes before slicing carefully.

Q SAVVY

My friends at Rollin Smoke Barbecue in Las Vegas stuff their meatloaf with shredded smoked meat.

Bacon-Wrapped Cherry Turkey Breasts

MAKES: 12 servings • **PREP:** 30 minutes • **SOAK:** overnight • **BRINE:** 2 hours • **COOK:** 1 hour

Turkey's not just for Christmas or Thanksgiving. With easy-to-fix turkey breasts readily available year-round, we should all be grilling them more often. Cooking bacon-wrapped turkey breasts on a maple plank adds a serious punch of flavor.

Basic Brine (page 14)

2 boneless, skinless turkey breasts (each 1½ lb)

1 tsp poultry seasoning

Kosher salt and finely ground black pepper to taste

1 lb thinly sliced bacon

1 sugar maple plank, soaked overnight

Cherry-Chipotle BBQ Sauce (page 37)

1. Prepare the brine and submerge the turkey breasts in it for 2 hours. **2.** Prepare the grill for direct cooking and preheat it to medium-high (375°F to 450°F). **3.** Remove the turkey breasts from the brine and pat dry on paper towels. Discard the brine. **4.** Sprinkle the turkey breasts with poultry seasoning and salt and pepper to taste. **5.** Wrap each turkey breast in half of the bacon, overlapping the slices slightly and tucking the ends under the thinner parts of the breast. Place the breasts on the soaked plank. Have ready a spritz bottle filled with water. **6.** Grill the turkey breasts until the internal temperature reaches 165°F, about 1 hour. Keep a close eye on the plank, as it may catch fire; spritz the plank with water if necessary. **7.** For the last 5 minutes of cooking, glaze the turkey breasts with the sauce. **8.** Remove the plank from the grill, tent the turkey breasts loosely with foil and let rest for 10 minutes before slicing.

Q SAVVY

One Thanksgiving, I was short on time and substituted this recipe for a whole bird. There were no complaints from the family. The turkey breasts were tender, moist and juicy, and the leftovers made great sandwiches the next day.

From-Texas-with-Love Beef Ribs (page 131)

BEEF
IT UP

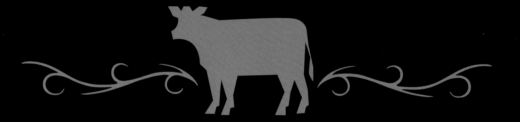

From stuffed burgers to award-winning brisket to mighty prime rib, beef is king of the grill. Try these meat-lover recipes and see why beef reigns supreme.

Shiitake Chuck Roast

MAKES: 16 servings • **PREP:** 30 minutes • **MARINATE:** at least 4 hours • **COOK:** 3 to 5 hours

Dried mushrooms are heavy on umami—the so-called fifth taste, after sweet, salty, sour and bitter—and, in this recipe, they add a punch of flavor to economical chuck roasts. Use a clean coffee grinder to grind the dried mushrooms to a powder.

2 boneless beef chuck roasts or bottom sirloin roasts (each about 4 lb)

Hickory wood chips

Oak wood chips

4 cups low-sodium beef stock

2 white sweet onions, slivered

Marinade

1 cup extra virgin olive oil

½ cup dried shiitake mushroom powder (about 2 cups dried mushrooms)

½ cup finely chopped fresh rosemary leaves

¼ cup low-sodium soy sauce

¼ cup finely chopped fresh thyme leaves

¼ cup finely chopped fresh oregano

¼ cup horseradish mustard

2 tbsp minced garlic

2 tbsp granulated onion (see page 25)

2 tbsp coarsely ground black pepper (butcher grind)

2 tsp kosher salt

1. Combine all the marinade ingredients in a very large bowl. Add the roasts, turning to coat well with the marinade. Cover the bowl with plastic wrap and refrigerate for at least 4 hours or overnight, turning the roasts at least once during marinating time. **2.** Prepare your smoker or grill for indirect cooking and preheat it to 225°F. Add a handful each of hickory and oak chips, following the instructions on page 9 for your type of smoker or grill. **3.** When the chips start to smoke, remove the roasts from the marinade and place on the cool side of the grill. Baste the roasts with the remaining marinade. **4.** Smoke the roasts until the internal temperature reaches 175°F, 2 to 3 hours. Replenish the wood chips by adding another handful every hour while the roasts cook. Remove the roasts from the grill. (Leave the grill on.) **5.** Place each roast in a disposable aluminum pan and add 2 cups stock and half of the slivered onions to each pan. Cover each pan tightly with heavy-duty foil. **6.** Place the pans on the cool side of the grill and cook until the internal temperature reaches 205°F and the meat starts to fall apart easily, 1 to 2 hours. **7.** Remove the roasts from the pans, tent loosely with foil and let rest for 15 minutes before slicing. Skim the fat from the cooking juices and serve the juices with the meat.

Q SAVVY

This recipe takes the chuck roasts to the tender pot-roast stage. If you prefer a rarer roast, smoke the chuck roasts just until the internal temperature reaches 120°F, 1½ to 2 hours. Remove the roasts from the grill, tent loosely with foil and let rest for 15 minutes before slicing.

180 Brisket

MAKES: 12 to 14 servings • **PREP:** stand (injection) 1 hour, marinate (brisket) 30 minutes, rest (flat) 1 hour • **COOK:** $10^1/_2$ to $12^1/_2$ hours • **REST:** 1 hour

In Kansas City Barbecue Society competitions, 180 is a perfect score, and that is what I was awarded when I served this brisket at a contest in Collingwood, ON. Doing brisket right takes practice, but once you nail it, there's nothing finer to serve to family and friends. Use a clean coffee grinder to grind the dried mushrooms to a powder.

1 whole beef brisket (14 to 16 lb)

¼ cup granulated onion (see page 25)

2 tbsp finely ground dried porcini mushrooms

¾ to 1 cup Montreal Steak Spice (page 26)

Hickory wood chips

Oak wood chips

Injection

2 cups bottled low-sodium water

¾ cup Butcher BBQ Prime Brisket Injection (see page 265)

Brisket Spritz

2 cups low-sodium beef stock

¾ cup Worcestershire sauce

2 tbsp fish sauce

Brisket Wrap

1½ cups low-sodium beef stock

1 medium white sweet onion, sliced

2 tbsp unsalted butter

1 tbsp coarsely ground black pepper (butcher grind)

1 tbsp Minor's Beef Au Jus Concentrate or concentrated beef bouillon

Glaze

½ cup Smoky Mountain Smokers Chipotle BBQ Sauce (see page 265)

1. Trim the top fat and silver skin from the brisket. The meat side (known as the flat) of the brisket should be completely exposed, with no visible fat. Trim the fat from the point of the brisket to expose the meat. Trim enough of the bottom fat cap to make the brisket as level as possible. **2.** Whisk together the injection ingredients in a medium bowl. Set aside for 1 hour. Fill the injector with the mixture. **3.** Inject the brisket at 1-inch intervals, injecting ½ oz each time. Continue to inject until the brisket starts pushing out more liquid than it is taking in. **4.** Mix together the granulated onion and ground mushrooms in a small bowl. Sprinkle the mixture over the meat of the brisket, coating it well. Sprinkle the meat of the brisket generously with steak spice, coating it well. **5.** Set the brisket aside at room temperature for 30 minutes before smoking. **6.** Prepare your smoker or grill for indirect cooking and preheat it to 180°F. Add a handful each of hickory and oak chips, following the instructions on page XX for your type of smoker or grill. When the chips start to smoke, place the brisket, fat side down, on the cool side of the grill. Smoke the brisket for 1 hour. **7.** Mix together all the spritz ingredients in a small bowl. Pour into a spray bottle. After the brisket has smoked for 1 hour, spray it all over with the spritz, ensuring the surface is damp but not dripping. **8.** Replenish the wood chips by adding another handful each of hickory and oak chips. Smoke the brisket for another 4 hours, replenishing the wood chips and spritzing the brisket every hour. **9.** After 4 hours, increase the grill temperature to 275°F. Add a handful of hickory chips. Smoke the brisket, without turning it, until the bark on the surface of the brisket has crusted, another 2 to 3 hours. **10.** While the brisket is cooking, mix together all the wrap ingredients in a small saucepan. Bring to a simmer, stirring until the concentrate has melted. Let cool to room temperature.

11. Remove the brisket from the grill and place, fat side down, on a double layer of heavy-duty foil large enough to wrap the brisket. (Leave the grill on.) **12.** Bring the foil up around the brisket. Pour the wrap mixture over the brisket, then seal the foil tightly around the brisket so none of the wrap leaks out. **13.** Return the foil-wrapped brisket to the grill. Continue to grill until the internal temperature of the brisket reaches 205°F, 2 to 3 hours. Remove the brisket from the grill. (Leave the grill on.) **14.** Carefully open the foil. Pour the juices into a small bowl. To make the glaze, add the barbecue sauce to the juices and mix well. **15.** Separate the flat (the leaner part) of the brisket from the point (the fattier end), where it splits naturally. Brush one-quarter of the glaze onto the flat. Wrap the flat in a double layer of plastic wrap, then in a layer of heavy-duty foil. Place the foil-wrapped flat in a cooler or a very large plastic container and cover with towels. Let the flat rest for at least 1 hour. **16.** Cut the point of the brisket into 1-inch cubes. These are known as burnt ends. Place the burnt ends in a disposable aluminum pan and toss with just enough glaze to coat them lightly. (Depending on the size of the brisket, you may not need all the glaze.) **17.** Increase the temperature of the grill to 275°F. Return the pan of burnt ends to the cool side of the grill. Cook the burnt ends for 1 hour, then, using tongs, flip them and spray with the spritz. Cook until the burnt ends are softened and the glaze has caramelized, about 30 minutes. **18.** Unwrap the flat of the brisket. Cut into slices against the grain. Serve with burnt ends.

Asian-Marinated Korean Beef Ribs

MAKES: 4 servings • **PREP:** 20 minutes • **MARINATE:** overnight • **COOK:** 8 to 10 minutes

Thinly cut Korean-style beef ribs are a cinch to grill, and the aromas from the Asian-inspired marinade will have your guests salivating. Pile the grilled ribs on a cutting board and let everyone have at 'em. Before you know it, you'll need to grill another batch.

4 lb Korean-style beef short ribs

Marinade
¾ cup low-sodium soy sauce
½ cup packed light brown sugar
½ cup rice wine vinegar
½ cup hoisin sauce
½ cup water
2 tbsp toasted sesame oil
2 tbsp minced garlic
1 tbsp minced fresh ginger
1 tbsp granulated onion (see page 25)

Garnish
2 tsp sesame seeds
2 green onions, chopped

1. Place the short ribs in a 1-gallon resealable freezer bag. **2.** Whisk together all the marinade ingredients in a medium bowl. Pour the marinade over the ribs, then seal the bag, squeezing to remove as much air as possible. Refrigerate overnight, turning the bag once or twice to ensure even distribution of the marinade. **3.** Prepare your grill for direct cooking and preheat it to medium-high (375°F to 450°F). **4.** Remove the ribs from the bag, discarding the remaining marinade. Grill the ribs, turning often, until slightly charred, 8 to 10 minutes. Serve sprinkled with sesame seeds and green onions.

Sunday Night Herb-Crusted Prime Rib (page 130)

Sunday Night
Herb-Crusted Prime Rib Photo on page 129

MAKES: 10 to 12 servings • **PREP:** 15 minutes • **MARINATE:** 4 hours • **COOK:** 1 to 1¾ hours

Everyone needs a go-to Sunday dinner that brings the whole family or a group of friends to the table. And this is mine. The herb crust adds extra flavor to the succulent prime rib, and the recipe comes together effortlessly. What more can you ask of a Sunday dinner?

¼ cup fresh rosemary leaves
¼ cup fresh flat-leaf parsley leaves
¼ cup minced garlic
¼ cup canola oil
3 tbsp Dijon mustard
2 tbsp kosher salt
2 tbsp finely ground black pepper
1 prime rib roast (5 to 7 lb)

1. Combine the rosemary, parsley, garlic, oil, mustard, salt and pepper in a food processor. Pulse until the herbs are finely chopped and the ingredients are combined. **2.** Coat the entire prime rib with the herb mixture. Refrigerate, uncovered, for 4 hours. **3.** Prepare your grill for indirect cooking and preheat it to 250°F. Place the prime rib, bone side down, on the cool side of the grill. **4.** Grill, allowing 12 to 15 minutes per pound, until the internal temperature of the thickest part of the prime rib reaches 120°F to 130°F for rare to medium-rare, 1 to 1¾ hours. **5.** Remove the prime rib from the grill, tent loosely with foil and let rest for 15 minutes before slicing.

Q SAVVY

The leftover prime rib makes an amazing filling for quesadillas.

Bear's Smokehouse Old-Fashioned

1 tsp superfine or fruit sugar
2 dashes Angostura bitters
1 tsp water
1 slice orange
Ice
2 oz Forty Creek or your favorite Canadian whisky
Orange twist for garnish
2 drained maraschino cherries

MAKES: 1 serving • **PREP:** 5 minutes

On Sunday night—or any night, for that matter—this old-fashioned teams well with roast beef.

1. Place the sugar in an old-fashioned glass. Add the bitters and water. Add the orange slice and muddle. **2.** Fill the glass with ice and add the whisky. Stir until the sugar has dissolved. **3.** Garnish with an orange twist and maraschino cherries.

From-Texas-with-Love Beef Ribs

MAKES: 2 servings • **PREP:** 20 minutes • **COOK:** 5 to 6 hours   **Photo on page 122**

Dear Texas: you rock. I have had some of the most mouthwatering, smoky beef ribs at Black's Barbecue, in Lockhart; Louie Mueller Barbecue, in Taylor; and John Mueller Meat Co. and La Barbecue, in Austin. Buy the meatiest beef ribs you can find for this recipe.

1 large rack Texas-size beef ribs
   (4 to 5 lb)
¾ cup Montreal Steak Spice (page 26)
Hickory wood chips
Mesquite wood chips

Spritz
2 cups best-quality beef stock
½ cup Worcestershire sauce

1. Prepare your smoker or grill for indirect cooking and preheat it to 225°F to 250°F. Add a handful each of hickory and mesquite chips, following the instructions on page 9 for your type of smoker or grill. **2.** Pull off the membrane from the bony side of the ribs (see sidebar, page 92). Season both sides of the ribs generously with the steak spice. **3.** Mix together the spritz ingredients and pour into a spray bottle. **4.** When the chips start to smoke, place the ribs, bone side down, on the cool side of the grill. **5.** Smoke the ribs until the meat has pulled back from the bones and is tender, 5 to 6 hours. Spray the ribs with the spritz every 30 to 45 minutes; replenish the wood chips by adding another handful every hour while the ribs smoke.

Double-Tied Beef Tenderloin

MAKES: 12 servings • **PREP:** 20 minutes • **COOK:** 43 to 55 minutes

Delicate tenderloin is a refined cut of beef that's truly an indulgence. Since it's very lean, beef tenderloin should never be cooked to more than medium, so have a digital thermometer on hand to ensure the beef doesn't overcook. Pair it with a glass of good red wine, and enjoy.

2 whole trimmed beef tenderloins
   (each 3 lb)
¼ cup Worcestershire sauce
¼ cup Montreal Steak Spice (page 26)
1 tsp rubbed dried thyme leaves
1 tsp dried rosemary
1 tsp dried dill weed

1. Lay one beef tenderloin on top of the other so the thick end of one lies over the thinner end of the other. Tie the beef tenderloins together at intervals with butcher twine (or ask your butcher to do this for you). **2.** Coat the tied tenderloins with Worcestershire sauce. Sprinkle evenly with the steak spice and herbs. Set aside. **3.** Prepare your grill for indirect cooking and preheat it to medium-high (375°F to 450°F). **4.** Grill the tenderloins on the hot side of the grill for 4 to 5 minutes per side until crusted. **5.** Move the tenderloins to the cool side of the grill. Continue to grill until the internal temperature of each tenderloin is 120°F to 130°F for rare to medium-rare, 35 to 45 minutes. **6.** Remove the tenderloins from the grill, tent loosely with foil and let rest for 10 to 15 minutes before slicing.

Rosemary-Garlic Marinated Flank Steak

MAKES: 6 servings • **PREP:** 20 minutes • **MARINATE:** overnight • **COOK:** 10 to 12 minutes

Flank steak is the ugly duckling of the steak world. It isn't nearly as sexy as a porterhouse, nor as attractive as a rib eye. But what flank lacks in beauty, it sure makes up for in flavor. Flank steak needs a marinade, but is an economical cut that can feed a lot of people when it's sliced thinly across the grain.

1 flank steak (about 2 lb)
Sea salt for serving

Marinade

1 cup soy sauce

½ cup rice wine vinegar

¼ cup finely chopped fresh rosemary leaves

2 tbsp minced garlic

2 tbsp sorghum syrup (see sidebar)

1 tbsp granulated onion (see page 25)

1 tbsp coarsely ground black pepper (butcher grind)

1. Mix together all the marinade ingredients in a medium bowl. Place the flank steak in a 1-gallon resealable freezer bag. Pour the marinade over the flank steak, then seal the bag, squeezing to remove as much air as possible. **2.** Refrigerate overnight, turning the bag once or twice to ensure even distribution of the marinade. **3.** Prepare your grill for direct cooking and preheat it to medium-high (375°F to 450°F). **4.** Remove the flank steak from the marinade, discarding the remaining marinade. Grill the flank steak, turning once, until the internal temperature reaches 120°F to 130°F for rare to medium-rare, about 10 to 12 minutes. (Flank steaks can vary in thickness, so keep an eye on the steak and don't overcook it; flank is best served rare to medium-rare.) **5.** Remove the flank steak from the grill, tent loosely with foil and let rest for 10 minutes. Slice thinly across the grain. I like to sprinkle the slices with sea salt just before serving.

Q SAVVY

Although referred to as sorghum "molasses" in the southern United States, sorghum syrup is actually made from sorghum grass, not sugar cane. It's an amber, mild-flavored syrup that's slightly sweeter than true molasses. Substitute maple syrup if you can't find it.

Top a salad with thinly sliced flank steak, or use it to stuff tacos.

Marinated Flap Steak Sandwich

MAKES: 6 servings • **PREP:** 15 minutes • **MARINATE:** at least 4 hours • **COOK:** 20 to 25 minutes

Flap steaks, cut from the bottom sirloin, are super versatile. I use them for kebabs, in tacos and for this easy sammie. I was thinking of Philly cheese steaks when I came up with this crowd-pleasing recipe. If you find it challenging to trim the silver skin from the steaks, ask your butcher to do it for you.

2 flap steaks, trimmed of silver skin (each about 2 lb)

Canola oil for oiling

1 each sweet red, yellow and green peppers, seeded and cut in half

1 red onion, cut in half

1 baguette, split horizontally

½ cup unsalted butter, softened

Kosher salt and finely ground black pepper to taste

1 cup shredded cheddar

Marinade

½ cup soy sauce

¼ cup minced garlic

2 tbsp molasses

½ tsp finely ground black pepper

1. Place the flap steaks in a 1-gallon resealable freezer bag.
2. Whisk together all the marinade ingredients in a small bowl until the molasses has dissolved. Pour the marinade over the steaks, then seal the bag, squeezing to remove as much air as possible. Refrigerate for at least 4 hours or overnight, turning the bag once or twice to ensure even distribution of the marinade.
3. Prepare your grill for direct cooking and preheat it to medium-high (375°F to 450°F). Generously oil the grill grates. 4. Place the peppers and onion on the grill. Grill, turning once, until softened, 6 to 8 minutes. Remove the peppers and onion from the grill. Cut into slices and set aside. 5. Remove the flap steaks from the bag, discarding any remaining marinade. Grill the steaks, turning once, until lightly charred and the internal temperature reaches 120°F to 130°F for rare to medium-rare, 6 to 8 minutes. 6. Remove the steaks from the grill, tent loosely with foil and let rest for 10 minutes.
7. While the steaks are resting, spread the cut sides of the baguette with butter. Grill, butter side down, until lightly toasted. (Leave the grill on.) 8. Place the steaks on the bottom half of the baguette and sprinkle with salt and pepper to taste. Top the steaks with the grilled peppers and onion. Sprinkle evenly with cheddar. Replace the top of the baguette. 9. Return the sandwich to the top rack or a cooler part of the grill until the cheese melts, 5 to 6 minutes. 10. Remove the sandwich from the grill, cut into slices and serve.

Smokin' Good Beef Bologna

MAKES: 12 servings • **PREP:** 20 minutes • **COOK:** 2½ hours

I grew up eating bologna sandwiches, but I never gave much thought to bologna and barbecue until I visited Cozy Corner Bar-B-Q in Memphis, TN. I tried the restaurant's slab of succulent smoked bologna and was hooked. Smoked bologna is all sorts of awesome on its own, so doesn't need anything fancy. Slice it thinly and serve on plain white bread with lots of great mustard.

1 chub all-beef bologna (3 lb)
½ cup spicy deli mustard
¼ cup Kansas City Rub (page 25)
Hickory wood chips
1 cup Diva Q Competition Sauce (page 33)
Sliced white bread
Additional mustard to serve

1. Remove the wax coating, if any, from the bologna. Score the outside of the bologna into ½-inch slices. Rub the bologna with the mustard, then sprinkle with the rub. **2.** Prepare your smoker or grill for indirect cooking and preheat it to 250°F. Add a small handful of hickory chips, following the instructions on page 9 for your type of smoker or grill. **3.** When the chips start to smoke, place the bologna on the cool side of the grill. Smoke the bologna until the internal temperature reaches 160°F, about 2 hours. Replenish the hickory chips by adding another small handful every 30 minutes while the bologna smokes. **4.** Slather the bologna with the Diva Q barbecue sauce. Smoke until the bologna has darkened and the sauce has set, about 30 minutes. **5.** Remove the bologna from the grill. Cut into slices at the score marks and serve on white bread with additional mustard.

Stuffed-to-the-Max Burgers

MAKES: 8 servings • **PREP:** 20 minutes • **CHILL:** at least 1 hour • **COOK:** 12 to 14 minutes

There are a million ways to make burgers, but this is burger nirvana. Stuffed burgers done my way, with a rolling pin and pizza wheel—really!—are easy to prep. Get your kids to help you and share the burger love.

3 lb ground beef (80% lean, 20% fat)

3 cloves garlic, minced

Kosher salt and finely ground black pepper to taste

Canola oil for oiling

8 kaiser buns, split

¼ cup salted butter, softened

Stuffing

½ cup bacon jam (see sidebar)

½ cup caramelized onions

2 cups grated sharp cheddar

Additional cheese for melting (optional)

Toppings

Cooked bacon, sliced cheese, lettuce leaves, good-quality mayonnaise (such as Hellmann's or Duke's), Homemade Smoked Ketchup (page 39) and/or mustard

1. Gently mix together the ground beef, garlic, and salt and pepper to taste in a large bowl. **2.** Lay a large sheet of plastic wrap on your work surface. Tip the ground beef mixture onto the plastic wrap. Using a rolling pin, flatten the ground beef out evenly on the plastic wrap to form a rectangle about ½ inch thick. **3.** Using a pizza wheel, score the rectangle of ground beef into 16 even-size squares. **4.** Top the 8 squares nearest to you with equal amounts of bacon jam, caramelized onions and cheddar. **5.** Grasp the edge of the plastic wrap furthest away from you and fold the top 8 burgers over the ones nearest to you. **6.** Peel the plastic wrap off the top of the burgers. Cut through the score marks with the pizza wheel to form 8 square burgers. **7.** With your hands, form each square burger into a round patty, making sure the edges of each burger are sealed to keep the stuffing in. Refrigerate the burgers for at least 1 hour before grilling. **8.** Prepare your grill for direct cooking and preheat it to medium-high (375°F to 450°F). Generously oil the grill grates. **9.** Season the burgers with salt and pepper to taste. Grill, turning once, until the internal temperature reaches 160°F, 12 to 14 minutes. For the last few minutes of cooking, top the burgers with additional cheese (if using). **10.** Remove the burgers from the grill, tent loosely with foil and let rest for 5 to 10 minutes before serving. **11.** While the burgers rest, spread the cut sides of the buns with butter. Grill, cut sides down, until golden. Assemble the burgers, adding your choice of toppings.

Q SAVVY

Bacon jam is readily available in almost any grocery store. It's fun to have on hand as it adds some really special, bacon-y goodness to this dish.

Q SAVVY

You can stuff the burgers with anything from herbed cream cheese to leftover pulled pork. Let your imagination run wild.

Rib Eye Tacos

MAKES: 6 servings • **PREP:** 30 minutes • **COOK:** 25 to 30 minutes

Tacos are everywhere, but these ones, chock full of greens, zesty salsa and rib eye—yes, rib eye—steak are satisfyingly over the top.

4 rib eye steaks (1½ inches thick)
12 flour tortillas
3 cups shredded napa cabbage

Fresh Tomato Salsa

8 oz roma tomatoes, seeded and chopped
2 jalapeños, seeded and finely diced
2 limes, zested
2 green onions, chopped
¼ cup finely chopped fresh cilantro
1 tsp kosher salt

Fresh Pineapple Salsa

Half fresh pineapple, peeled, cored and chopped
½ cup finely chopped red onion
¼ cup finely chopped fresh cilantro
1 tsp kosher salt

1. Mix all the ingredients for each salsa in 2 separate medium serving bowls. Set aside for at least 10 minutes before serving. **2.** Grill the steaks according to the recipe for Reverse-Seared Steaks (page 21). **3.** Remove the steaks from the grill, tent loosely with foil and let rest for 5 to 10 minutes before slicing into thin strips. **4.** Fill each tortilla with napa cabbage, steak and a salsa of your choice.

Q SAVVY

On a carb-free kick? Serve the steak and salsas on a bed of organic greens.

Gail-a-Rita

2 bottles (each 64 oz/1.9 L) Daily's Cocktails Peach or Raspberry Mix or 15 cups peach or raspberry juice
2 bottles (each 64 oz/1.9 L) white grape and peach or white grape and raspberry juice
2 bottles (40 oz/1.14 L) tequila
1 bottle (26 oz/750 mL) triple sec
Ice
Raspberries or sliced peaches for garnish
Bendy straws

MAKES: about 2¾ gallons (30 servings) • **PREP:** 10 minutes

Gail Gurney-Smith of The 5th Artery Barbeque Team from Amherst, NY, came up with this margarita recipe at a competition in 2012. She made a big batch in a 3-gallon cooler and served it up to all her fellow competitors. Get in the spirit by wearing sombreros and fake moustaches (if necessary!) and fixing a mess of tacos to go with it. You can use really inexpensive tequila for this.

1. Pour the mix, juice, tequila and triple sec into a clean, sanitized 3-gallon cooler and stir well. **2.** Ladle over ice into red plastic Solo cups. Garnish with raspberries or peach slices and serve with bendy straws.

Meat Cake

MAKES: 12 to 14 servings • **PREP:** 30 minutes • **CHILL:** 2 hours • **COOK:** about 1 hour

You have to be a little bit barbecue-obsessed to make a birthday cake out of meat, but this recipe is all sorts of yum. The first time I made it, the wow factor was so high I started to get requests from friends. One year I even made heart-shaped ones for Valentine's Day.

Cakes

2 lb ground chuck

2 lb Italian sausage, casings removed

8 oz bacon, ground

1 cup panko bread crumbs

1 medium onion, minced

2 eggs, beaten

3 jalapeños, seeded and minced

¼ cup Sriracha sauce

1 tbsp Montreal Steak Spice (page 26)

1 tbsp minced garlic

Kosher salt and finely ground black pepper to taste

Cherry wood chips

Hickory wood chips

3 cups shredded cold-smoked cheddar (page 18)

Icing

6 to 7 cups hot cooked, mashed potatoes

Barbecue sauce in a squeeze bottle, for writing

1. Gently mix together the ground chuck, sausage, bacon, bread crumbs, onion, eggs, jalapeños, Sriracha sauce, steak spice, garlic, and salt and pepper to taste in a large bowl. **2.** Divide the meat mixture between two 8-inch round baking pans, smoothing it out so it's level. Refrigerate for 2 hours. **3.** Prepare your smoker or grill for indirect cooking and preheat it to 250°F. Add a small handful each of cherry and hickory chips, following the instructions on page 9 for your type of smoker or grill. **4.** When the chips start to smoke, place the pans on the cool side of the grill. Smoke until the internal temperature of each cake reaches 150°F, 45 to 60 minutes. Replenish the wood chips by adding another handful halfway through the smoking time. **5.** Remove the pans from the grill and drain off any excess fat. (Leave the grill on.) Carefully remove the cakes from the pans. Top each cake evenly with cheese. **6.** Place the cakes, cheese side up, on the cool side of the grill. Cook until the internal temperature of each cake reaches 160°F, about 15 minutes. **7.** Remove the cakes from the grill and place one cake on a serving plate. Top the cake with half of the hot mashed potato. Place the second cake on top of the potato. Spread the top of the cake with the remaining mashed potato. **8.** Use the barbecue sauce to drizzle a message on the top of the cake. Serve immediately.

> ## Q SAVVY
> *If you're feeling creative, spoon any leftover mashed potato into a piping bag fitted with a large tip and pipe mashed-potato flowers and other decorations on top of the cake.*

Smoked Bone Marrow

MAKES: 4 servings • **PREP:** 15 minutes • **COOK:** 15 to 20 minutes

If someone had once told me that I would happily scrape out the innards of a bone and slather it on toast, I'd have said they were crazy. These days I'm hooked. Smoked bone marrow has the same characteristics as top-notch pâté. It's pure beef fat—no diet food here—and its superb flavor is enhanced by smoking. Ask your butcher to cut the marrow bones in half lengthwise.

Hickory wood chips

8 beef marrow bones, cut in half lengthwise

¼ cup Montreal Steak Spice (page 26)

½ cup finely chopped fresh flat-leaf parsley

1 baguette, sliced and toasted

1. Prepare your smoker or grill for indirect cooking and preheat it to 375°F to 450°F. Add a handful of hickory wood chips, following the instructions on page 9 for your type of smoker or grill. **2.** Season the marrow side of the bones with steak spice. **3.** When the wood chips start to smoke heavily, place the bones, cut sides up, on the cool side of the grill. **4.** Smoke the marrow bones until the marrow becomes gelatinous, 15 to 20 minutes. Watch the bones carefully; if you grill them for too long, the marrow will liquefy and run out of the bones. **5.** Carefully remove the bones from the grill, scrape the marrow out of the bones and spread it onto the baguette toasts, sprinkle with parsley and serve.

> **Q SAVVY**
>
> Once you've enjoyed the marrow, do what my friends Patrick Weir, Jess Sweeney and chef Dave Mottershall do: scrub the bones and use them as whiskey luges. Put one end of a bone in your mouth, then pour whiskey in the other end.

Brie and Spinach-Stuffed Chicken Breasts (page 159)

FOWL PLAY

Forget all about dried-out chicken, duck or turkey on the grill.
These recipes bring succulent, juicy poultry with big,
bold flavors right into your backyard.

Smoked Crispy Duck

MAKES: 6 servings • **PREP:** 30 minutes • **COOK:** about 2¾ hours

My sister-in-smoke Angie Quaale took me out for lunch when I was visiting her in Vancouver. Angie is a dynamo of a woman with great taste in food. That day we ate terrific shredded duck with hoisin sauce in lettuce wraps. Here's my take on that crispy, succulent duck. The shredded meat is also wonderful in tacos, or portion out the duck and serve as a main course.

1 duck (about 5 lb), spatchcocked (see sidebar)
Kosher salt and finely ground black pepper to taste
Hickory wood chips

Glaze

¾ cup maltose syrup (see sidebar), honey or molasses
½ cup low-sodium soy sauce
2 tbsp grated fresh ginger
2 tsp minced garlic
1 tsp five-spice powder
1 tsp finely ground black pepper
½ tsp kosher salt

1. Rinse the duck and pat it dry with paper towels. Use your fingers to separate the skin from the breast, then, with a very sharp knife, slash the breasts of the duck. (This will help render out more fat.) Sprinkle the duck with salt and pepper. 2. Prepare your smoker or grill for indirect cooking and preheat it to 225°F. If using a gas or charcoal grill, place a disposable aluminum pan directly on the coals or burners on the cool side of the grill to catch the fat that will drip off the duck. 3. Add a handful of hickory chips, following the instructions on page 9 for your type of smoker or grill. 4. When the chips start to smoke, place the duck, skin side up, on the cool side of the grill (directly over the aluminum pan if using a charcoal or gas grill). Smoke the duck for 2 hours. Replenish the wood chips by adding another handful every 30 minutes while the duck smokes. 5. Mix together all the ingredients for the glaze in a small bowl. 6. After 2 hours, increase the temperature of the grill to 300°F. Glaze the duck with some of the maltose mixture. Smoke the duck, glazing it every 10 minutes, until the glaze is used up, 30 to 40 minutes. 7. Increase the temperature of the grill to high (450°F-plus). Smoke until the duck is a rich dark color, the skin is crisp and the internal temperature of the thickest part of the thigh reaches 175°F, about 10 minutes. 8. Remove the duck from the grill and let rest, uncovered, for 20 minutes. 9. When the duck is cool enough to handle, divide it into portions or shred the duck meat, chopping up the crispy skin and mixing it in with the meat.

Q SAVVY

Maltose syrup is used in beer- and bread-making. Look for it in home brewing supply stores, health food stores or Asian groceries.

Pineapple Stand Chicken

MAKES: 6 to 8 servings • **PREP:** 30 minutes • **COOK:** 40 to 50 minutes

Beer-can chicken is *so* last year. It's also a waste of perfectly drinkable beer. My version, which stands the chicken on a fresh pineapple, adds just as much juiciness plus some tropical flavor.

1 large pineapple

1 chicken (3 to 4 lb)

¼ cup Diva Q Pork and Chicken Rub (page 24)

Fresh Pineapple Salsa (page 140)

. . . .

Q SAVVY

The pineapple stand for the chicken can be prepared ahead of time, but don't invert the chicken onto it until just before grilling. There are enzymes in pineapple that can break down the meat and make it mushy if the fruit comes in contact with the chicken too far in advance.

. . . .

1. Trim the top from the pineapple. Cut a slice from the bottom of the pineapple so it stands level. **2.** With the pineapple standing upright on a cutting board and using a large, sharp knife, cut the peel and any "eyes" from the pineapple. **3.** Cut vertical slices of flesh from the pineapple all around the core, stopping 2 inches from the base of the pineapple. You'll be left with the vertical core of the pineapple on a 2-inch base, and this forms your "stand" for the chicken. Reserve the pineapple for the salsa. **4.** Prepare your grill for indirect cooking and preheat it to 275°F. **5.** Season the chicken inside and out lightly with the rub. Invert the chicken onto the pineapple stand. **6.** Place the chicken on its pineapple stand on the cool side of the grill. Grill for 20 minutes. Rotate the chicken and grill until the internal temperature of the breast reaches 165°F and the thigh reaches 175°F, 20 to 30 minutes. **7.** Remove the chicken from the grill and remove the pineapple stand. Tent the chicken loosely with foil and let rest for 10 minutes before serving with the salsa.

Get Your Jerk On!

MAKES: 6 to 8 servings • **PREP:** 20 minutes • **MARINATE:** overnight • **COOK:** 45 to 55 minutes

Crank up the Bob Marley tunes and get your Jamaican groove on with this easy jerk chicken that's perfect for a backyard gathering. For the most authentic jerk, check out the sidebar. Ya, mon.

1 large chicken (4 to 5 lb)
Canola oil for oiling

Marinade

1 small red onion, minced

¼ cup chopped green onions

¼ cup canola oil

2 to 4 scotch bonnet peppers, minced

2 small jalapeños, minced

3 tbsp Appleton Estate or your favorite amber rum

2 tsp finely ground white pepper

2 tsp kosher salt

1½ tsp ground thyme

½ tsp ground allspice

½ tsp grated nutmeg

½ tsp cinnamon

1. Combine all marinade ingredients in a food processor and pulse until smooth. 2. Place the chicken in a resealable 2-gallon freezer bag. Pour the marinade into the bag, turning to coat the chicken with the marinade. Squeeze out as much air as possible from the bag, seal the bag and refrigerate overnight. 3. Prepare your grill for indirect cooking and preheat it to 350°F. 4. Remove the chicken from the bag, discarding the marinade. Generously oil the grill grates. Place the chicken, breast side up, on the cool side of the grill and grill for 15 to 20 minutes. 5. Rotate the chicken, then grill for another 15 to 20 minutes. 6. Flip the chicken over, then grill until the internal temperature reaches 165°F in the breast and 175°F in the thigh, about 15 minutes. For crispier skin, move the chicken to the hot side of the grill for the last few minutes of cooking. 7. Remove the chicken from the grill, tent loosely with foil and let rest for 10 minutes before serving.

Q SAVVY

Try the jerk marinade on pork or salmon, too. Marinate the pork overnight, but the salmon for just 30 minutes.

For the most authentic jerk chicken, grill it over pimento wood charcoal, made from the wood of the Jamaican allspice tree. (Look for pimento wood charcoal at your local barbecue supply store.) Fill a chimney starter with the charcoal and light it. When all the charcoal is covered with gray ash, pour out the coals and spread them evenly over half of your grill. The bottom and top vents should be open halfway. Follow the grilling directions in the recipe.

Herbed Tuscan Bricked Chicken

MAKES: 6 to 8 servings • **PREP:** 20 minutes • **MARINATE:** at least 4 hours • **COOK:** 40 to 50 minutes

One day I'll get to Italy to eat *pollo al mattone*. Until then I'll be content with my version of what translates as Tuscan bricked chicken. The brick presses the chicken into the grill grates so it cooks more evenly and quickly and becomes crunchy, juicy and packed full of flavor. If you don't have any bricks, use a heavy cast iron skillet. I have a small herb garden in my backyard, and I change up the herbs in this recipe depending on what's in season.

1 lemon, zested and juiced

1 tbsp finely chopped fresh oregano

1 tbsp finely chopped fresh marjoram

1 tbsp finely chopped fresh flat-leaf parsley

1 tbsp minced garlic

2 tsp finely chopped fresh rosemary leaves

1 chicken (3 to 4 lb), spatchcocked (see page 148)

¼ cup extra virgin olive oil

Kosher salt and finely ground black pepper to taste

2 standard building bricks

Lemon wedges for garnish

1. Mix together the lemon zest and juice, oregano, marjoram, parsley, garlic and rosemary. **2.** Rub the chicken all over with the oil and then with the lemon mixture, making sure to rub some of it under the skin of the breast meat. **3.** Season the chicken with salt and pepper to taste. Cover the chicken with plastic wrap and refrigerate for at least 4 hours or overnight. **4.** Prepare your grill for direct cooking and preheat it to medium-low (300°F). **5.** Wrap the bricks in heavy-duty foil to cover them completely. **6.** Place the chicken, skin side down, on the grill. Immediately place the bricks on top of the chicken. Grill until the skin is crispy, 15 to 20 minutes. Flip the chicken and grill until the internal temperature of the breast meat reaches 165°F and the thigh reaches 175°F, 25 to 30 minutes. **7.** Remove the chicken from the grill, tent loosely with foil and let rest for 10 minutes. Serve the chicken with lemon wedges on the side.

Roadside Chicken

MAKES: 6 to 8 servings • **PREP:** 20 minutes • **COOK:** about 1 hour

When I'm driving through the southern United States, I often pass gas stations where some dude is out front fixing barbecue and basting chicken. This is my take on some incredible chicken I've enjoyed at the side of the road. I love that you can putter at the grill while you baste this chicken, adding layers of flavor each time. Make a couple of batches—your tummy will thank you for the leftovers.

Canola oil for oiling

1 large chicken (4 to 5 lb), cut into 8 portions

3 large navel oranges, cut in half

Baste

1 cup apple cider vinegar

½ cup canola oil

¼ cup orange juice with pulp

¼ cup Worcestershire sauce

2 tbsp granulated sugar

1 tbsp chili powder

1 tbsp garlic powder

1 tsp kosher salt

1 tsp finely ground black pepper

Q SAVVY

A dash of hot sauce in the baste adds a kick of spice to the chicken.

1. Prepare your grill for indirect cooking and preheat it to 275°F to 300°F. **2.** Whisk together all the baste ingredients in a nonmetallic bowl, whisking until the sugar has dissolved and the spices are well mixed. **3.** Generously oil the grill grates. Place the chicken pieces, skin side up, on the cool side of the grill and brush with the baste. **4.** Grill the chicken, basting every 10 minutes and turning the pieces occasionally, until the internal temperature of the breast pieces reaches 165°F and the thighs and legs reaches 175°F, about 50 minutes. **5.** Remove the chicken from the grill, tent loosely with foil and let rest for 10 minutes. **6.** While the chicken is resting, grill the orange halves, cut sides down, on the hot side of the grill. **7.** Serve the chicken with segments of grilled orange.

Spicy Curry Chicken Skewers

MAKES: 4 servings • **PREP:** 30 minutes • **MARINATE:** at least 2 hours • **COOK:** 8 to 12 minutes

As a busy mom of three mighty munchkins, I'm always in search of quick midweek grills. This fragrant curried chicken is an easy recipe that everyone enjoys. Use a little or a lot of curry and vary the heat level, according to what your family likes. Serve the skewers over couscous, or slide the meat off the skewers and tuck in a pita or flatbread.

¼ cup canola oil

3 tbsp minced garlic

2 tbsp mild curry powder

2 tbsp Spicy Thai Rub (page 28)

1 tsp finely ground black pepper

2 lb skinless, boneless chicken breasts, cut into 1-inch chunks

4 to 6 metal skewers

Cucumber-Yogurt Dip

2 English cucumbers, seeded and cubed

1 cup Greek yogurt

2 tsp finely chopped fresh dill

1 tbsp freshly squeezed lemon juice

2 cloves Smoked Garlic (page 15), smashed

Kosher salt and finely ground black pepper to taste

1. Mix together the oil, garlic, curry powder, Thai rub and black pepper in a medium nonmetallic bowl. Add the chicken and toss to coat with the oil mixture. Cover and refrigerate for at least 2 hours or overnight. 2. Mix together all the dip ingredients in a medium bowl. Cover and refrigerate for at least two hours. 3. Prepare your grill for direct cooking and preheat it to medium-high (375°F to 450°F). 4. Thread the chicken onto the skewers. Place the chicken skewers on the grill and grill, turning once, until the internal temperature reaches 165°F, 8 to 12 minutes. 5. Remove the skewers from the grill and serve with the Cucumber-Yogurt Dip.

Q SAVVY

I've served these skewers as an appetizer for a dinner party and used the spice rub on whole chicken breasts.

Brie and Spinach-Stuffed Chicken Breasts

Photo on page 146

MAKES: 4 servings • **PREP:** 15 minutes • **BRINE:** 1 hour • **COOK:** 8 to 10 minutes

So elegant and refined, this is ladies-who-lunch stuffed chicken. The stuffing can be switched up with things you already have in your fridge, but my family loves the combo of spinach and brie. If you like, slice the chicken and serve it in a bun, or let cool and use to fix a posh chicken salad.

Basic Brine (page 14)

4 boneless, skinless chicken breasts

Kosher salt and finely ground black pepper to taste

4 oz brie, sliced and rind removed

1 cup packed baby spinach leaves

4 small, slim metal skewers

Moroccan Spice Rub (page 29)

Canola oil for oiling

1. Prepare the brine and submerge the chicken breasts for 1 hour. 2. Remove the chicken breasts and pat dry on paper towels. Discard the brine. 3. Cut a horizontal slit in the side of each chicken breast to create a pocket. Season each pocket with salt and pepper to taste. Put 1 slice of brie and one-quarter of the spinach leaves in each pocket. Secure each pocket with a skewer. Season the outside of the breasts with the rub. 4. Prepare your grill for direct cooking and preheat it to medium-high (375°F to 450°F). Generously oil the grill grates. Grill the chicken breasts, turning often, until the internal temperature reaches 165°F, 8 to 10 minutes. 5. Remove the chicken from the grill, tent loosely with foil and let rest for 10 minutes before serving.

Sweet and Sassy Chicken Lollipops

MAKES: 6 servings • **PREP:** 45 minutes • **COOK:** 30 to 45 minutes

I like having a handle on chicken, and these lollipops are fun to look at and taste great. I've made chicken lollipops for competitions, on TV shows and for my family, and they're always a real crowd-pleaser.

1 cup Diva Q Competition Sauce (page 33)

¼ cup Sriracha sauce

2 lb chicken drumsticks

¼ cup Diva Q Pork and Chicken Rub (page 24)

1 tsp chipotle powder

Canola oil for oiling

1. Mix together the Diva Q sauce and Sriracha sauce in a small bowl. Set aside. 2. With a small, sharp knife, cut around the thin, bony end of each chicken drumstick, cutting through the skin, meat and tendons until you reach the bone. Push the meat and skin down toward the thick end of the drumstick to form a "lollipop." Repeat with the remaining drumsticks. 3. Generously sprinkle the drumsticks with the rub and chipotle powder. 4. Prepare your grill for direct cooking and preheat it to medium-high (375°F to 450°F). Generously oil the grill grates. 5. Grill the chicken, turning often, until the internal temperature reaches 175°F, 20 to 30 minutes. 6. Glaze the chicken with the sauce mixture. Grill, turning often, until the glaze sets, 10 to 15 minutes. 7. Remove the chicken from the grill, tent loosely with foil and let rest for 10 minutes before serving.

Q'n Canucks' Take-Out-the-Competition Punch

1 bottle (26 oz/750 mL) vodka

1 bottle (26 oz/750 mL) dark, golden or white rum

16 oz banana liqueur

16 oz tequila

8 cups soda water

4 cups cranberry juice

4 limes, thinly sliced

Ice

MAKES: about 1½ gallons (30 servings) • **PREP:** 10 minutes

The award-winning Q'n Canucks BBQ Team from Guelph, ON, always serves up batches of this knock-you-on-your-butt punch at barbecue competitions. I love it with the Sweet and Sassy Chicken Lollipops.

1. Mix together the vodka, rum, liqueur and tequila in a large drink dispenser or punch bowl. 2. Add the soda water, cranberry juice, lime slices and lots of ice.

Q SAVVY

If you like, wrap the exposed bone of each chicken drumstick in foil before grilling to protect it from the glaze. Make sure to remove the foil before serving.

Competition Chicken Thighs

MAKES: 4 servings • **PREP:** 45 minutes • **MARINATE:** 15 minutes • **COOK:** about 1½ hours

When it comes to barbecue competitions, chicken is hard work. Teams spend more time on chicken than on any other meat, making sure each piece is uniform and removing all the fat. Before one contest, I played with chicken recipes for two weeks straight, serving chicken thighs for every meal. My family didn't appreciate it, but I ended up with a great recipe that pleased the judges at the competition. You'll need an eight-cavity mini loaf pan and a wire rack for this recipe.

8 bone-in, skin-on chicken thighs

½ cup Diva Q Pork and Chicken Rub, finely ground (page 24)

Hickory wood chips

Butter-flavor cooking spray

½ cup low-sodium turkey stock (see sidebar)

½ cup unsalted butter

1 tsp MSG

2 cups Diva Q Competition Sauce (page 33)

¼ cup Texas Pepper Jelly Cherry Habanero Jelly or your favorite pepper jelly

Q SAVVY

Since this is a competition recipe, I've listed the exact ingredients I used on the day, but at home, you could use low-sodium chicken stock, if you prefer. And, just in case you do try competing, recipes like this look great in a parsley- or lettuce-lined turn-in box, spritzed with warm water at the last minute for a high-shine finish.

1. Trim the chicken thighs so they are a uniform shape and size, removing any hard pockets of fat or veins from the undersides of the thighs. 2. Peel the skin back from the chicken thighs without removing it completely. Sprinkle the flesh of the chicken thighs on both sides with the rub. Replace the skin and let the chicken thighs rest at room temperature for 15 minutes. 3. Prepare your smoker or grill for indirect cooking and preheat it to 250°F. Add a small handful of hickory chips, following the instructions on page 9 for your type of smoker or grill. 4. Spray an eight-cavity mini loaf pan generously with cooking spray. Pour 1 tbsp stock into each cavity of the loaf pan. 5. Carefully place a chicken thigh, skin side up, in each cavity. Divide the butter into 8 even-size pieces and place one piece on each thigh. 6. When the hickory chips start to smoke, place the pan of chicken on the cool side of the grill. Smoke for 45 minutes. 7. Flip the chicken thighs over and cover the pan tightly with heavy-duty foil. Return the pan to the cool side of the grill and smoke until the internal temperature reaches 175°F, about 30 minutes. 8. Remove the pan from the grill. Carefully remove the chicken thighs to a wire rack set over a rimmed baking sheet. Pour the juices out of the loaf pan into a small bowl. Add the MSG. Mix well and set aside. Pour the Diva Q sauce over the chicken thighs. Return the thighs to the cool side of the grill. Smoke until the sauce is set, 15 to 20 minutes. 9. Remove the chicken thighs from the grill and brush the underside of each thigh with a thin layer of pepper jelly. 10. Pour the reserved loaf-pan juices into an injector and inject each chicken thigh with juices, inserting the needle through the side of each chicken thigh. 11. Remove the chicken thighs from the grill and serve.

Blue-Ribbon Wings

MAKES: 4 to 6 appetizer servings • **PREP:** 25 minutes • **MARINATE:** overnight • **COOK:** about 1½ hours

Even more fun than entering a barbecue competition is winning it. This is the recipe that garnered the top spot in the Tyson Best Wing on the Planet competition for our team—twice. I use commercial sauces for the glaze because you don't always have to make everything from scratch. But feel free to use your own favorite combo. Serve the wings with plenty of napkins and beer.

2½ lb chicken wings (about 24)

1 bottle (5 oz/142 mL) Tabasco chipotle sauce

Hickory wood chips

Canola oil for oiling

Wing Rub

2 tbsp sweet smoked paprika

1 tbsp chili powder

2 tsp kosher salt

2 tsp garlic powder

2 tsp granulated sugar

2 tsp mild curry powder

2 tsp hot mustard powder

1 tsp finely ground black pepper

1 tsp ground cumin

1 tsp chipotle powder

Glaze

1 cup Frank's RedHot Sweet Chili Sauce

¼ cup Sweet Baby Ray's Original Barbecue Sauce

1. Place the chicken wings in a 1-gallon resealable freezer bag and pour the Tabasco over them, tossing to coat evenly. Seal the bag and refrigerate overnight, turning after a couple of hours to evenly distribute the marinade. 2. Remove the chicken wings from the bag, discarding the Tabasco. Place the chicken wings on a rimmed baking sheet. 3. Mix together all the rub ingredients in a small bowl. Sprinkle the rub on both sides of the chicken wings. 4. Prepare your smoker or grill for indirect cooking and preheat it to 225°F to 250°F. Add a handful of hickory chips, following the instructions on page 9 for your type of smoker or grill. 5. When the chips start to smoke, place the chicken wings on the grill and smoke them for 1 hour. Flip the chicken wings and continue to smoke them until the internal temperature reaches 165°F, 30 minutes. Replenish the wood chips by adding another handful every 30 minutes while the chicken wings smoke. 6. Remove the chicken wings from the grill and place in a large bowl. (Leave the grill on). 7. Mix together the glaze ingredients in a microwave-safe bowl. Microwave for 1 minute on high power. 8. Reserving ¼ cup of the glaze to serve as a dipping sauce, pour the remaining glaze over the chicken wings and toss to coat evenly. 9. Increase the temperature of the smoker or grill to medium-high (375°F to 450°F) and oil the grill grates. 10. Place the glazed chicken wings on the hot side of the grill and grill, turning once, until the glaze has caramelized, 2 to 4 minutes. 11. Remove the chicken wings from the grill and serve with the remaining glaze on the side for dipping.

Game Day Shredded Buffalo Chicken Sammie

MAKES: 6 servings • **PREP:** 20 minutes • **COOK:** about 12 minutes

Sometimes guests can't help but cancel dinner at the last minute. Friends had a last-minute emergency when I was planning to cook them Roadside Chicken. The next day, I reconfigured the chicken into one heck of a sandwich, and this recipe was born. I now make Roadside Chicken just so I can fix the sammie.

1 baguette

¾ cup unsalted butter, melted

1½ cups shredded pepper Jack or cold-smoked cheddar (page 18)

½ cup Diva Q Competition Sauce (page 33)

½ cup Piri Piri Hot Sauce (page 34)

1 freshly cooked, hot Roadside Chicken (page 156)

Additional Diva Q Competition Sauce and/or Piri Piri Hot Sauce to serve

1. Prepare your grill for direct cooking and preheat it to medium-high (375°F to 450°F). 2. Slice the baguette in half lengthwise. Brush the cut sides with some of the butter. Grill the baguette, cut sides down, until lightly toasted. 3. Remove the baguette from the grill and sprinkle the cheese on the cut sides. Return the baguette, cheese side up, to the upper shelf of the grill. Grill until the cheese is melted, 5 to 8 minutes. 4. Mix together the remaining butter and Diva Q and Piri Piri sauces in a large bowl. 5. Shred the chicken, removing the skin and bones. Add the meat to the sauce mixture and toss well. Pile the chicken high on the toasted baguette. Serve with additional sauce, if you like.

Q SAVVY

This recipe is required eating when watching a football game. Beer and whiskey (for the grown-ups) are also a must.

Mutha Chicken's Slaughterhouse Slammer

1 cup root beer

3 oz Captain Morgan or your favorite amber rum

Ice

Pinch of grated nutmeg

MAKES: 1 serving • **PREP:** 3 minutes

My dear friend Dan McGrath (aka Mutha Chicken) owns Galvinell Meat Co. in Conowingo, MD. After a long day in the slaughterhouse, he likes to wind down with this unique combo of root beer and rum. Me? I team it with my Buffalo Chicken Sammie.

1. Pour the root beer and rum into a tall glass. 2. Add the ice and nutmeg and stir to combine.

Grilled Greek Turkey Burgers

MAKES: 12 servings • **PREP:** 30 minutes • **COOK:** 12 to 14 minutes

Lean turkey burgers can sometimes taste like cardboard. My healthy—yet satisfying—burgers are made nice and moist by the addition of grated onion.

Dilled Tzatziki

2 cups plain Greek yogurt

1 cup crumbled feta cheese

2 tsp dried dill weed

2 lemons, zested and juiced

Kosher salt and finely ground black pepper to taste

Burgers

3 lb ground turkey

¾ cup minced pitted kalamata olives

1 medium white sweet onion, finely grated

2 lemons, zested

2 tbsp Greek Rub (page 28)

2 cloves garlic, minced

Kosher salt and finely ground black pepper to taste

Canola oil for oiling

To Serve

12 whole wheat hamburger buns, split

½ cup unsalted butter, melted

Curly leaf lettuce leaves, pitted kalamata olives and sliced red onion

1. Mix together all the ingredients for the dilled tzatziki in a medium bowl. Refrigerate until ready to serve. 2. For the burgers, gently mix together the ground turkey, olives, onion, lemon zest, rub, garlic, and salt and pepper to taste in a large bowl. Form the mixture into 12 even-size patties. 3. Prepare your grill for direct cooking and preheat it to medium-high (375°F to 450°F). Generously oil the grill grates. 4. Grill the burgers until the internal temperature reaches 165°F, 6 to 7 minutes per side. 5. Brush the cut sides of the buns with melted butter. Grill, cut side down and turning often, until golden. 6. Assemble the burgers, topping each with dilled tzatziki, lettuce, black olives and red onion.

Q SAVVY

The burger mix makes fantastic meatballs, too. Just form the turkey mixture into balls and thread onto metal skewers.

Cajun-Butter-Injected Turkey Breast

MAKES: 4 to 6 servings • **PREP:** 30 minutes • **MARINATE:** at least 4 hours • **COOK:** 16 to 20 minutes

Injecting a turkey breast with Cajun-spiked butter ensures moist, juicy meat. Wrapping the breast in plastic wrap before injecting it prevents any splash back from the injection. You may want to double up this recipe because the leftovers taste fantastic.

1 boneless turkey breast (about 3 lb)
1 tbsp canola oil
Cajun Rub (page 25)

Injection

1 cup apple juice
1 tbsp concentrated shrimp and crab boil (see sidebar)
½ cup honey
½ cup clarified unsalted butter (see page 76)
2 tbsp Cajun Rub (page 25)

1. Whisk together all the injection ingredients in a small saucepan. Bring to a boil, stirring to dissolve the honey. Remove the saucepan from the heat and let cool completely. **2.** Cover the turkey breast with a piece of plastic wrap. Fill an injector with three-quarters of the apple juice mixture. Inject the mixture through the plastic wrap into the turkey breast, making multiple injections. Reserve the remaining apple juice mixture. **3.** Remove the plastic wrap from the turkey breast and rub it lightly with oil. Sprinkle the turkey breast with the rub. Cover and refrigerate for at least 4 hours or overnight. **4.** Prepare your grill for direct cooking and preheat it to medium (300°F to 375°F). **5.** Grill the turkey breast, turning once, until the internal temperature of the thickest part reaches 165°F, 16 to 20 minutes. **6.** Remove the turkey breast from the grill. Fill a clean injector with the remaining apple juice mixture. Inject the mixture into the hot turkey breast. Tent the turkey breast loosely with foil and let rest for 5 to 10 minutes before slicing.

Q SAVVY

Concentrated shrimp and crab boil is a liquid seasoning traditionally used to flavor the cooking water for a Cajun-style seafood boil. Look for it in the spice aisle of larger supermarkets.

Slashed Crispy Orange-Glazed Trout (page 172)

GONE FISHIN'

Catch of the day hits the grill. From succulent scallops to heavenly halibut, get the scoop on how to cook all your favorites. No fishing poles required.

Slashed Crispy Orange-Glazed Trout

MAKES: 4 to 6 servings • **PREP:** 20 minutes • **COOK:** about 20 minutes

Photo on page 170

Grilling whole fish is incredibly simple. My fishmonger, Johnny, rocks. He advises me on which fish and seafood work best on the grill and explains how to clean them. Slashing the sides of trout in this recipe seriously cuts down on the grilling time. The orange and lime slices help keep the fish moist.

2 whole trout (each about 3 lb), cleaned

Kosher salt and finely ground pepper to taste

2 navel oranges, sliced

2 limes, sliced

Canola oil, for oiling

Glaze

1 tsp toasted sesame oil

Half red onion, finely chopped

2 navel oranges, zested and juiced

3 tbsp sweet chili sauce

2 tbsp fish sauce

3 dried kaffir lime leaves

Half stalk bruised lemongrass (see page 98)

1. Prepare your grill for direct cooking and preheat it to medium-high (375°F to 450°F). **2.** Cut several slashes in both sides of each trout. Season the inside of each fish with salt and pepper. Stuff each fish with orange and lime slices. Set aside. **3.** Heat the sesame oil in a small saucepan over medium heat. Sauté the onion until softened but not browned. **4.** Add the orange zest and juice, chili sauce, fish sauce, lime leaves and lemongrass. Bring to a boil. Let boil until reduced by half. **5.** Strain the glaze through a fine-mesh sieve, discarding the solids. Set aside. **6.** Generously oil the grill grates several times. Grill the trout on one side for 5 to 6 minutes. Carefully flip the trout over. Grill until the skin is crispy, 5 to 6 minutes, brushing with the glaze for the last couple of minutes.

Blackened Cajun Salmon

MAKES: 6 to 8 servings • **PREP:** 15 minutes • **COOK:** 10 to 20 minutes

When I first heard the term "blackened" in relation to food, I wondered why people would want their food burnt. Now, many years later and a (little) bit wiser, I am a fan of these Cajun-based blackening seasonings, which add so much to fish and chicken. Usually blackening involves a cast iron skillet and butter, but I have adapted the method for the grill. The brown sugar enhances the sweetness of the salmon, but you can omit it if you prefer.

1 whole boneless side of salmon with skin

Cajun Rub (page 25)

2 tbsp packed dark brown sugar

Canola oil for oiling

1 lemon, quartered

1. Prepare your grill for direct cooking and preheat it to medium-high (375°F to 450°F). **2.** Mix together the rub and sugar in a small bowl. Generously season the flesh side of the salmon. **3.** Generously oil the grill grates. Grill the salmon, skin side down, until the salmon is firm to the touch and the flesh flakes easily, 10 to 20 minutes. (The grilling time will vary depending on the thickness of the salmon. Keep an eye on it and don't walk away from your grill.) **4.** Carefully remove the salmon to a platter and squeeze the lemon quarters overtop.

Q SAVVY

For easier flipping, put your trout in a fish-grilling basket, but make sure to spray the basket several times first with nonstick cooking spray.

Q SAVVY

Any leftover salmon is great on sandwiches the following day. Just remove the skin, flake the flesh with a fork and add mayonnaise, capers and seasonings to taste.

Salmon Burgers with Tartar Sauce

MAKES: 4 servings • **PREP:** 30 minutes • **COOK:** 12 to 14 minutes

These simple salmon patties are perfect for a hot day, served with white wine and a green salad.

Lemony Tartar Sauce

½ cup good-quality mayonnaise

2 tbsp drained, minced gherkins

1 tbsp drained capers

1 tbsp apple cider vinegar

1 tbsp honey Dijon mustard

1 tsp grated lemon zest

1 tsp freshly squeezed lemon juice

Burgers

1 lb minced boneless, skinless salmon

1 egg

2 tbsp minced fresh chives

1 tbsp grated lemon zest

1 tbsp Dijon mustard

½ tsp cayenne

Kosher salt and finely ground black pepper to taste

¾ cup panko bread crumbs (approx.)

Canola oil for oiling

Brioche buns

1. Mix together all the ingredients for the tartar sauce in a small bowl. Cover and refrigerate until ready to serve. **2.** Prepare your grill for direct cooking and preheat it to medium-high (375°F to 450°F). **3.** Mix together the salmon, egg, chives, lemon zest, mustard, cayenne, and salt and pepper to taste in a medium bowl. Add just enough bread crumbs so the mixture holds together (you may not need all the crumbs). Form the mixture into 4 even-size patties. **4.** Generously oil the grill grates. Grill the patties, turning often, until golden brown and firm to the touch, 12 to 14 minutes. **5.** Remove the patties from the grill. Serve in the brioche buns with the tartar sauce.

Mahi Mahi Sliders

MAKES: 6 servings • **PREP:** 20 minutes • **COOK:** 6 to 8 minutes

My parents had a place in Florida for many years, and I have many happy fishing—and grilling—memories from that time. I like to season fish generously before grilling it, and Old Bay, a combo of celery salt, spices and paprika, does the trick here.

6 boneless, skinless mahi mahi fillets (each about 4 oz)

1 tbsp Old Bay Seasoning

½ tsp finely ground black pepper

Canola oil for oiling

6 ciabatta buns, split and toasted

Cowboy Caviar (page 222)

Curly leaf lettuce

Lemony Tartar Sauce (page 174)

1. Prepare your grill for direct cooking and preheat it to medium-high (375°F to 450°F). **2.** Sprinkle the mahi mahi fillets with Old Bay Seasoning and pepper. **3.** Generously oil the grill grates. Grill the mahi mahi, turning once, until just firm to the touch, 6 to 8 minutes. **4.** Serve the mahi mahi on toasted ciabatta buns and top with Cowboy Caviar, lettuce and tartar sauce.

Q SAVVY

For the Mahi Mahi Sliders, any firm fish works well in this recipe. Just be sure your grill is clean and well oiled so the fish doesn't stick.

Grilled Tuna Steak Tacos

MAKES: 6 servings • **PREP:** 15 minutes • **COOK:** 4 to 6 minutes

There is a reason tacos proliferate on menus everywhere: they're super tasty and easy to make. Just make sure you don't overcook the tuna—ahi tuna deserves your attention and just a light grilling to medium-rare at most. If you are on a gluten-free or carb-reduced diet, skip the tortillas and serve the tuna on a bed of mixed greens.

4 ahi tuna steaks (each 1½ inches thick)
¼ cup canola oil
2 tbsp Montreal Steak Spice (page 26)
Additional canola oil for oiling
12 flour tortillas (6-inch)
4 cups Creamy Carrot Slaw (page 232)
4 limes, quartered

1. Prepare your grill for direct cooking and preheat it to medium-high (375°F to 450°F). **2.** Brush the tuna steaks with canola oil and sprinkle with steak spice. **3.** Generously oil the grill grates. Grill the tuna, turning once, just until lightly charred but still medium-rare, 4 to 6 minutes. **4.** Remove the tuna from the grill and cut it crosswise into thin slices. **5.** Top each tortilla with tuna slices and Creamy Carrot Slaw and serve with lime wedges.

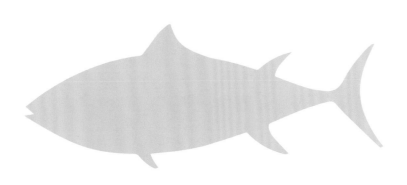

Just for the Halibut

MAKES: 4 servings • **PREP:** 30 minutes • **COOK:** 6 to 8 minutes

When you start with a really great piece of fish, you don't need to add a lot to it. Photographer Ken Goodman came up with this delicious sauce when we were shooting the food for this book. He's also a trained chef, so whipped the sauce up in minutes. It pairs perfectly with the halibut.

Canola oil for oiling

4 boneless, skinless halibut steaks
    (1 ½ inches thick)

¼ cup sunflower oil

2 tbsp Spicy Thai Rub (page 28)

1 lime, quartered

Ken's Green Sauce

½ cup firmly packed fresh basil leaves

½ cup firmly packed fresh mint leaves

2 tbsp freshly squeezed lime juice

1 clove garlic

½ cup extra virgin olive oil

Water, as needed

Kosher salt and finely ground black
    pepper to taste

1. For Ken's Green Sauce, place the basil, mint, lime juice and garlic in a blender or a food processor. Pulse until finely minced and combined. **2.** With the motor running, pour in the oil, blending until smooth. Add a little water, if necessary, if the sauce is too thick. Scrape into a small bowl and season with salt and pepper to taste. **3.** Prepare your grill for direct cooking and preheat it to medium-high (375°F to 450°F). **4.** Generously oil the grill grates several times. Brush each halibut steak on both sides with sunflower oil. Season each lightly with the Thai rub. **5.** Grill the halibut, turning once, until just starting to become opaque, 6 to 8 minutes. **6.** Remove the halibut from the grill and serve with Ken's Green Sauce and lime wedges.

Q SAVVY

When buying fish, it's a good idea to know your fishmonger and to buy sustainable seafood from a trusted source. When I'm in Canada I love dealing with 1 Fish 2 Fish in Langley, BC, and Johnny's Seafood in Barrie, ON.

Grilled Cilantro-Lime Halibut Skewers

MAKES: 4 servings • **PREP:** 20 minutes • **MARINATE:** 30 minutes • **COOK:** 12 to 15 minutes

A simple fresh marinade, brightened with lime and cilantro, and a light grilling brings out the lovely texture and sweet flavor of fresh halibut.

Marinade

¼ cup canola oil

¼ cup finely chopped fresh cilantro

2 tsp minced garlic

½ tsp chipotle powder

1 lime, zested and juiced

Kosher salt and finely ground black pepper to taste

Skewers

1½ lb boneless, skinless halibut, cut into 1-inch chunks

4 metal or soaked bamboo skewers

2 sweet green peppers, seeded and cut into 1-inch chunks

8 oz yellow and red cherry tomatoes

Lime wedges for serving

1. Combine all the marinade ingredients in a large resealable freezer bag. Add the halibut, turning to coat with the marinade. Refrigerate for 30 minutes. **2.** Thread the halibut, sweet peppers and cherry tomatoes alternately onto the skewers. **3.** Prepare your grill for direct cooking and preheat it to medium-high (375°F to 450°F). **4.** Grill the skewers, turning often, until the fish is just firm to the touch, 12 to 15 minutes. Serve with lime wedges.

Q SAVVY

Any firm-fleshed fish—try cod, salmon or snapper—can be used for these kebabs.

Seafood Feast Pizza

MAKES: 4 servings • **PREP:** 30 minutes • **REST:** 1 hour • **COOK:** about 15 minutes

This is an exceptional homemade pizza and quite the change from pepperoni and cheese. The seafood is the star here and takes pizza from humble to haute. For more on grilling pizza, check out my Pizza Pointers on page 57.

1 lb pizza dough

6 large shrimp, peeled and deveined

½ tsp Cajun Rub (page 25)

6 littleneck clams in their shells, scrubbed

Cornmeal for dusting

6 asparagus stalks, cooked and chopped

2 to 3 lobster claws, steamed, shelled and meat cubed

White Sauce

1½ tbsp all-purpose flour

1½ tbsp salted butter, softened

½ cup whole milk

½ cup freshly grated Parmesan

2 cloves Smoked Garlic (page 15), minced

1 tbsp finely chopped fresh chives

Kosher salt and finely ground black pepper to taste

1. Prepare the dough as described in the Grilled Prosciutto, Olive and Mozzarella Pizza recipe (page 55). **2.** For the white sauce, whisk together the flour and butter in a small saucepan over medium heat. Cook, stirring often, for 2 minutes. **3.** Whisk in the milk until smooth. Stir in the Parmesan, garlic and chives. Cook, whisking constantly, until the sauce is bubbly and smooth. Remove from the heat, season with salt and pepper to taste and set aside. **4.** Prepare your grill for direct cooking and preheat it to medium-high (375°F to 450°F). Season the shrimp with Cajun rub. Grill the shrimp and clams until the clams open and the shrimp are opaque, 2 to 4 minutes. **5.** Prepare your grill for cooking the pizza as described in the Grilled Prosciutto, Olive and Mozzarella Pizza recipe (page 55). **6.** Top the pizza crust with white sauce, asparagus, clams, shrimp and lobster. Grill as described on page 55.

Grilled Lobster Feast

MAKES: 6 servings • **PREP:** 15 minutes • **FREEZE:** 30 minutes • **COOK:** 20 to 22 minutes

This is for those special occasions when you want to splurge big. Invite a bunch of friends over, cover the table with newspaper and indulge in a lobster feast. I like keeping things fairly simple so that nothing detracts from the lobsters' rich flavor, but grilled corn (page 194) is a must.

6 live lobsters (each 1½ lb)

¼ cup canola oil

Flavored Butters (page 16)

1. Numb the lobsters by freezing them for 30 minutes. **2.** Lay one lobster on its back. Insert the tip of a large chef's knife just below the large claws and, in one swift cut, slice vertically through the lobster's head. Repeat with the remaining lobsters. **3.** Prepare your grill for direct cooking and preheat it to medium-high (375°F to 450°F). **4.** Brush the lobsters with canola oil. Grill the lobsters, turning once, until the shells are bright red and white juices start to coagulate on the outer tail and joints of the lobsters and their internal temperature reaches 145°F, 20 to 22 minutes. **5.** Remove the lobsters from the grill and serve with Flavored Butters and lots of napkins.

Shrimp and Lobster–Stuffed Calamari

MAKES: 4 servings • **PREP:** 30 minutes • **COOK:** 8 to 12 minutes

When calamari are grilled right, they're delicate with nary a hint of rubber. The calamari tubes are the perfect shapes to stuff. I've used cooked sausage or fish, but this combo of lobster and shrimp take them over the top. Use smaller tubes for appetizers or serve larger ones—like in this version—as a main course.

1 cup chopped, cooked lobster meat

1 cup chopped, cooked, peeled shrimp

2 tbsp unsalted butter, melted

2 cloves Smoked Garlic (page 15), smashed

1 tbsp finely chopped fresh chives

1 tbsp hot sauce

8 calamari tubes (4 to 5 inches long), cleaned

Kosher salt and finely ground black pepper to taste

Canola oil for oiling

1. Prepare your grill for direct cooking and preheat it to medium-high (375°F to 450°F). **2.** Mix together the lobster, shrimp, butter, garlic, chives and hot sauce in a medium bowl. **3.** Stuff each calamari tube with the lobster mixture, making sure not to overfill the tubes. Season the tubes with salt and pepper to taste. **4.** Generously oil the grill grates. Grill the calamari, turning once, until they start to turn opaque, 8 to 12 minutes. Serve immediately.

Firecracker Prawns

MAKES: 4 servings • **PREP:** 10 minutes • **COOK:** 8 to 10 minutes

As their name suggests, these prawns are damn hot, but I think you need to push the envelope on heat once in a while. Easy to make, the prawns may be spicy but they're still really flavorful. To temper the heat a bit, stir ¼ cup melted butter into the Piri Piri Hot Sauce before adding the prawns. Make sure you have plenty of ice-cold beer to pair with these.

12 giant (about 3lb) prawns or shrimp in their shells, deveined
2 tbsp Spicy Thai Rub (page 28)
1 cup Piri Piri Hot Sauce (page 34)
4 Thai bird's-eye chilies, thinly sliced

1. Prepare your grill for direct cooking and preheat it to medium-high (375°F to 450°F). **2.** Sprinkle the prawns evenly with the Thai rub. Grill, turning once, until charred and the flesh is just turning opaque, 8 to 10 minutes. **3.** Remove the prawns from the grill and place in a large bowl. Add the piri piri sauce and toss well. Sprinkle with chilies and serve.

Buttery Garlic-Lemon Smoked Mussels

MAKES: 6 to 8 servings • **PREP:** 20 minutes • **COOK:** 30 to 45 minutes

You don't have to fuss with mussels much, which makes this one of the easiest dishes ever. It's the perfect appetizer for when you have lots of guests hanging out in your backyard for cocktails.

Hickory wood chips
4 lb mussels in their shells, scrubbed and debearded
1 cup salted butter, melted
¾ cup Riesling
¾ cup finely chopped shallots
6 cloves Smoked Garlic (page 15), smashed
¼ cup finely chopped fresh chives
2 lemons, zested and juiced
1 baguette, sliced and toasted
Additional lemon wedges for serving

1. Prepare your smoker or grill for indirect cooking and preheat it to 275°F. Add a handful of hickory chips, following the instructions on page 9 for your type of smoker or grill. **2.** Place the mussels in a disposable aluminum pan. When the chips start to smoke, place the pan on the cool side of the grill. **3.** Smoke until all the mussels have opened, 30 to 45 minutes. Discard any mussels that do not open. Remove the pan from the grill and tent it with foil. **4.** Meanwhile, whisk together the butter, Riesling, shallots and garlic in a small saucepan. Bring to a boil, then pour the butter mixture over the mussels. **5.** Scatter the mussels with chives and lemon zest, then drizzle with lemon juice. Serve with baguette toasts and lemon wedges.

Diva Oysters

MAKES: 4 servings • **PREP:** 30 minutes • **COOK:** 10 to 15 minutes

I have a fondness for oysters, whether raw, grilled, baked or broiled. Oysters, crayfish, bacon and a little bit of Parmesan are an outstanding combo. I think the culinary rule that says you can't put cheese with seafood is bull. All rules are made to be broken—especially when they try to stop something from tasting this good.

2 cups chopped frozen crayfish tail meat, thawed (see sidebar)

¾ cup crumbled, cooked bacon

½ cup freshly grated Parmesan, divided

½ cup panko bread crumbs

¼ cup unsalted butter, melted

3 cloves Smoked Garlic (page 15), finely chopped

3 tbsp finely chopped fresh chives

Kosher salt and finely ground black pepper to taste

12 oysters in their shells

12 whole crayfish (see sidebar)

1. Prepare your grill for direct cooking and preheat it to medium-high (375°F to 450°F). **2.** Mix together the crayfish meat, bacon, ¼ cup of the Parmesan, the bread crumbs, butter, garlic, chives, and salt and pepper to taste in a medium bowl. **3.** Shuck the oysters, loosening them from their bottom shells but leaving them in the shells. Add any liquor from the oysters to the crayfish mixture and stir well. **4.** Place the oysters on a baking sheet. Spoon the crayfish mixture on top of the oysters, dividing evenly. Sprinkle evenly with the remaining Parmesan. **5.** Place the oysters and the whole crayfish on the grill. Cook until the topping on the oysters is bubbling and beginning to brown and the whole crayfish are deep red, 10 to 15 minutes. **6.** Serve 3 oysters per person, topping each oyster with 1 whole crayfish.

Boucherie Pimm's Cup

7 thin slices cucumber, divided

2 tsp simple syrup (see note, right)

4 oz Pimm's No. 1

½ cup ginger ale

1 tsp freshly squeezed lemon juice

Crushed ice

MAKES: 1 serving • **PREP:** 5 minutes

I love the food at Boucherie in New Orleans. The restaurant's version of this classic libation is just made for my take on oysters. To make simple syrup, combine equal quantities of granulated sugar and water in a saucepan. Bring to a boil, stirring to dissolve the sugar, then cool completely. Simple syrup keeps for weeks in the fridge.

1. Muddle 6 of the cucumber slices with the simple syrup in a tall glass. **2.** Add the Pimm's, ginger ale and lemon juice and stir gently. **3.** Add the ice and garnish with the remaining cucumber slice.

Planked Scallops with Smoked Tomato-Garlic Oil

MAKES: 6 servings • **PREP:** 45 minutes • **COOK:** about 1 hour

These big, juicy scallops with a hint of smoke are terrific as an appetizer or main course. Make sure to smoke the scallops only until they are just starting to turn opaque or they'll be overcooked and rubbery. Any leftover smoked tomato oil can be used to drizzle on shrimp, pasta or grilled fish.

Apple wood chips

2 pints cherry tomatoes, cut in half

1 cup extra virgin olive oil

12 cloves Smoked Garlic (page 15)

3 sprigs fresh thyme

1 large white sweet onion, cut in half

12 fresh scallops (1¼ pounds)

6 cross-grain untreated alder wood planks

Kosher salt and finely ground black pepper to taste

3 tbsp finely chopped chives

1. Prepare your smoker or grill for indirect cooking and preheat it to 225°F to 250°F. Add two handfuls of apple chips, following the instructions on page 9 for your type of smoker or grill. **2.** Place the tomatoes, oil, garlic and thyme in a disposable aluminum pan. When the chips start to smoke, place the pan on the cool side of the grill. Also place the onion, cut sides down, on the cool side of the grill. **3.** Grill the tomatoes, stirring every 10 minutes, until they taste smoky and have begun to break down, about 40 minutes. Grill the onion, turning often, until lightly charred, about 10 to 12 minutes. Remove the pan and the onion from the grill when done. **4.** Increase the temperature of the grill to medium-high (375°F to 450°F). **5.** Place 2 scallops in the center of each plank. Drizzle 1 tablespoon of the tomato olive oil over each scallop and top each with a clove of smoked garlic. Sprinkle with salt and pepper to taste. **6.** Grill the planks on the hot side of the grill just until the scallops start to turn opaque, 15 to 20 minutes. **7.** Separate the smoked onion into layers. Sprinkle the scallops with chives and drizzle with additional tomato oil, then serve the scallops with the smoked tomatoes and garlic and pieces of smoked onion.

Q SAVVY

When grilling on wood planks over direct heat, have a spray bottle of water on hand to spritz the planks' edges if they catch on fire.

Scallops come in all shapes and sizes. They are usually sold using a range of numbers to describe how many scallops of a particular size would make up a pound. The smaller the number, the larger (by weight) the scallops are, for example U15 means it would take fewer than 15 scallops to make up a pound.

Seafood Celebration Chowder

MAKES: 6 to 8 servings • **PREP:** 25 minutes • **COOK:** 40 to 50 minutes

This isn't your everyday chowder. It's one of those dishes you'll remember for a lifetime. I love using a variety of seafood in this chowder. My favorite combo is shrimp, lobster, halibut, squid and mussels, but feel free to change it up. Just make sure to add the items that need the longest cooking first.

½ cup unsalted butter

½ cup onion, finely diced

½ cup carrot, finely diced

½ cup celery, finely diced

½ cup sweet green pepper, seeded and finely diced

2 tbsp saffron powder

2 tbsp Old Bay Seasoning

2 tsp chipotle powder

4 cups lobster stock

Hickory wood chips

8 very large (about 2 lb) shrimp, peeled and deveined

8 oz boneless, skinless halibut

1 cup water

3 tbsp cornstarch

1 cup whipping (heavy) cream

12 mussels in their shells

2 squid (each 3 to 4 inches), cleaned

2 lb lobster claws, steamed

Kosher salt and finely ground black pepper to taste

2 tbsp finely chopped fresh chives

1. Melt the butter in a large cast iron pot over medium heat. Sauté the onion, carrot, celery and green pepper until the onion is softened but not browned. **2.** Stir in the saffron powder, Old Bay Seasoning and chipotle powder. **3.** Add the stock and bring to a boil. Let boil for 5 to 10 minutes, then reduce the heat to a simmer. **4.** Prepare your smoker or grill for indirect cooking and preheat it to 225°F. Add a handful of hickory chips, following the instructions on page 9 for your type of smoker or grill. **5.** When the chips start to smoke, place the shrimp and halibut on the hot side of the grill. Cook until the shrimp and halibut are just starting to turn opaque, 10 to 15 minutes. Remove the shrimp and halibut from the grill and set aside. **6.** Place the cast iron pot containing the lobster stock mixture on the cool side of the grill. **7.** Whisk together the water and cornstarch in a small bowl and whisk into the lobster stock mixture. Whisk in the cream. **8.** Add the mussels and squid to the pot and bring to a simmer. Add the shrimp, halibut and lobster claws and simmer until all the mussels have opened and the squid is opaque, about 20 minutes. **9.** Remove the pot from the grill. Season the chowder with salt and pepper to taste. Sprinkle with chives and serve immediately.

Grilled Paneer and Charred Rapini (page 204)

SIZZLING SIDES
(AND A MEATLESS BURGER)

A gal can't live on meat alone. Luckily, a little kiss of smoke and flame can transform veggies, rice and even tofu from mundane to magnificent. There are recipes here, too, that don't use the grill but that go so well with barbecue, they're right at home in this book.

Grilled Corn Three Ways

MAKES: 4 servings • **PREP:** 30 minutes • **COOK:** 20 minutes

Corn is one of those gotta-have-it-or-it's-not-summer veggies, and we serve a lot of it at our house when it's in season. We set out tables covered in newsprint in our backyard and get all the kids involved in shucking the corn. Once it's ready, we serve the corn up on big platters with different toppings. Any of the Flavored Butters on page 16 are terrific on grilled corn. Here are some of our other favorites.

8 ears corn, husked and silk removed

Mexican Corn

¼ cup good-quality mayonnaise, such as Hellmann's or Duke's

1 tbsp ancho powder

1 cup grated Cotija cheese (see sidebar)

Kosher salt and finely ground black pepper to taste

2 limes, quartered

Chipotle-Lime Corn

¾ cup unsalted butter, melted

1 tbsp minced canned chipotles in adobo sauce●

3 limes, zested and juiced

Kosher salt and finely ground black pepper to taste

Traditional Corn

¾ cup unsalted butter, melted

Kosher salt and finely ground black pepper to taste

1. Bring a large pot of salted water to a boil. Add the corn and cook for 5 minutes. Drain well. **2.** Prepare your grill for direct cooking and preheat it to medium-high (375°F to 450°F). Grill the corn, turning often, until lightly charred, 15 minutes.

Mexican Corn: Mix together the mayonnaise and ancho powder in a small bowl. Brush the grilled corn all over with the mayonnaise mixture, then sprinkle with cheese and salt and pepper to taste. Serve with lime wedges.

Chipotle-Lime Corn: Mix together the butter and chipotles in a small bowl. Brush the grilled corn all over with the butter mixture, then sprinkle with lime zest and juice and salt and pepper to taste.

Traditional Corn: Brush the grilled corn all over with butter and serve with salt and pepper to taste.

> ## Q SAVVY
>
> *Cotija is a hard, salty cow's milk cheese from Mexico. Look for it in Latino grocery or specialty cheese stores.*
>
> *For a prettier presentation, peel the husk back from each ear of corn, then remove the silk. Use one leaf of the husk to tie the ends of the rest of the husk together, leaving the ear of corn exposed.*

Home-Style Creamed Grilled Corn

MAKES: 8 servings • **PREP:** 20 minutes • **COOK:** about 10 minutes

Here's an indulgent side dish that's as comforting as your favorite sweater and that pairs well with just about any meat off the barbecue. It's also a great way to use up leftover grilled corn. If your corn is super sweet, you can omit the sugar.

8 ears grilled corn (page 194)
½ cup unsalted butter
½ cup all-purpose flour
2 to 3 cups whole milk
½ cup minced shallots
1 tbsp granulated sugar
Pinch of freshly grated nutmeg
Kosher salt and finely ground black pepper to taste

1. With a large, sharp knife, slice the kernels from the ears of corn. Set aside. **2.** Melt the butter in a large saucepan over medium heat. Add the flour and cook, stirring, for 2 to 3 minutes. **3.** Gradually whisk in 2 cups of the milk, adding the milk ½ cup at a time. Cook, whisking constantly, until the sauce is smooth, thick and bubbly. **4.** Add the corn kernels, shallots, sugar and nutmeg, stirring to coat the kernels with the sauce. **5.** If the sauce is too thick, add more milk. Season with salt and pepper to taste. Serve hot or cold.

Q SAVVY

Mexican Creamed Grilled Corn Add 1 can (4½ oz/127 mL) chopped green chilies and 1 tsp fajita seasoning to the sauce along with the corn. Sprinkle the creamed corn with grated Cotija cheese (see sidebar, page 194).

Watermelon Mayhem

2 cups granulated organic coconut sugar
1 cup water
4 cups cubed peeled, seedless watermelon
2 cups coconut water
3 limes, zested and juiced
12 oz light rum
Crushed ice
Lime and watermelon wedges for garnish

MAKES: 6 servings • **PREP:** 20 minutes • **COOK:** 10 minutes

This ultimate hot-weather drink is a natural with all summer grills, but especially corn.

1. Mix together the coconut sugar and water in a small saucepan. Bring to a boil, stirring to dissolve the sugar. **2.** Reduce the heat and simmer until the coconut syrup is light golden, about 10 minutes. Remove the saucepan from the heat and let the syrup cool. Refrigerate until chilled. **3.** Purée the watermelon in a blender until smooth and frothy. Add the coconut water and lime zest and juice and blend to combine. **4.** Pour the watermelon mixture into a large pitcher. Add the rum and coconut syrup to taste. **5.** Pour into glasses over crushed ice and garnish with lime and watermelon wedges.

Smoked Sriracha-Butter Onion Blossoms

MAKES: 4 servings • **PREP:** 20 minutes • **COOK:** 1½ to 2 hours

This simple dish packs a big punch. Grilled onions with butter and garlicky, spicy Sriracha sauce are knock-it-out-of-the-park amazing. The longer you smoke the onions, the sweeter they become.

1 cup salted butter, softened

½ cup Sriracha sauce

4 white sweet onions

Kosher salt and finely ground black pepper to taste

Hickory wood chips

Shredded provolone (optional)

1. Blend together the butter and Sriracha sauce in a small bowl. **2.** Peel the onions, leaving the root ends intact. With a sharp knife, score a crosshatch pattern in the top of each onion, avoiding cutting right through the onions. **3.** Wrap the bottom half of each onion in foil. Sprinkle each onion with salt and pepper to taste. Spread the top of each onion with Sriracha butter, dividing evenly. **4.** Prepare your smoker or grill for indirect cooking and preheat it to 250°F. Add a handful of hickory chips, following the instructions on page 9 for your type of smoker or grill. **5.** Smoke the onions on the cool side of the grill until tender, 1½ to 2 hours. Replenish the wood chips by adding another handful to the grill every 30 minutes while the onions smoke. **6.** Just before the onions are ready, sprinkle each with provolone (if using). When the provolone is melted, remove the onions from the grill. Remove the foil and serve warm.

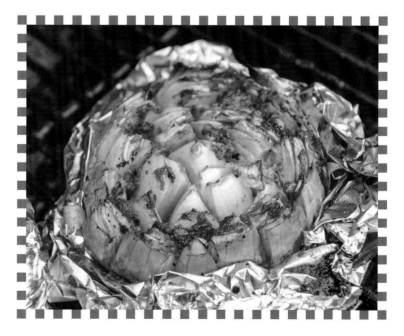

Candied Smoked Carrots

MAKES: 4 servings • **PREP:** 15 minutes • **COOK:** about 1½ hours

Team sugar, butter and spice with smoke and the combo transforms carrots into a spectacular side dish. Try this with parsnips or cubes of butternut squash, too.

2 lb baby carrots
½ cup packed light brown sugar
½ cup unsalted butter, melted
1 tsp five-spice powder
Kosher salt and finely ground black pepper to taste
Pecan wood chips

1. Toss together all the ingredients (except the wood chips) in a disposable aluminum pan. **2.** Prepare your smoker or grill for indirect cooking and preheat it to 225°F. Add a handful of pecan chips, following the instructions on page 9 for your type of smoker or grill. **3.** Place the pan of carrots on the cool side of the grill and smoke, turning the carrots every 15 minutes, until tender, about 1½ hours. Replenish the wood chips by adding another handful every 30 minutes while the carrots smoke. **4.** Remove the pan from the grill and serve the carrots warm.

Grilled Brussels Sprouts and Bacon

MAKES: 4 to 6 servings • **PREP:** 20 minutes • **COOK:** 30 to 40 minutes

I hated Brussels sprouts when I was a kid and always tried to get our dog to eat them for me. It never worked, and I was always the last one sitting at the kitchen table long after the meal was over. Now that I'm a grown-up, I've discovered that grilling and a little bacon make a world of difference to sprouts. The second my kids asked for more, I knew I was on to a winner.

2 lb Brussels sprouts, trimmed
¼ cup bacon fat, melted
Kosher salt and finely ground black pepper to taste
¼ cup birch syrup or maple syrup
6 slices bacon, cooked and crumbled

1. Toss together the Brussels sprouts, bacon fat, and salt and pepper to taste in a large bowl. **2.** Prepare your grill for direct cooking and preheat it to medium-high (375°F to 450°F). **3.** Put the sprouts in a vegetable grill basket. Grill, turning the sprouts often, until tender, 30 to 40 minutes. **4.** Tip the sprouts onto a serving platter. Drizzle with birch syrup and sprinkle with crumbled bacon.

Q SAVVY

Slice any leftover sprouts and serve in a salad the next day.

Collard Greens with Bacon

MAKES: 10 to 12 servings • **PREP:** 30 minutes • **COOK:** about 1¼ hours

I've had collard-greens cooking lessons from a few Southern cooks. Each has their own take on how to turn these tough greens into bowls of goodness. I like using a ham bone in my version because I love the combo of salty collard greens and peppery vinegar.

2 large bunches collard greens, washed

8 oz bacon, chopped

2 white sweet onions, finely chopped

1½ gallons cold water (approx.)

1 lb chopped double-smoked ham

1 ham bone

4 whole cloves garlic

2 tbsp unsalted butter

2 tbsp dehydrated sweet red pepper flakes

Kosher salt and finely ground black pepper to taste

Pepper vinegar to taste (see sidebar)

1. Chop the collard greens into bite-size pieces, discarding any tough stems. Set aside. **2.** Cook the bacon in a very large pot over medium heat until it's crispy. Using a slotted spoon, remove the bacon and drain on paper towels. Crumble the bacon finely and set aside. **3.** Add the onions to the fat remaining in the pot and sauté until softened but not browned. **4.** Add the water, chopped ham, ham bone, garlic, butter and red pepper flakes to the pot. Bring to a boil over high heat. Reduce the heat to medium-low and simmer, uncovered, for 15 minutes. **5.** Add the collard greens and more water, if necessary, to ensure the collard greens are covered. Bring back to a simmer. Cook, uncovered, until the collard greens are tender, about 45 to 60 minutes, depending on how thick the leaves are. **6.** Season with salt and pepper to taste. Serve the collard greens topped with the crumbled bacon and with pepper vinegar on the side.

Q SAVVY

Pepper vinegar is a spicy condiment popular in the southern United States, where it's sprinkled liberally over hearty greens like collards, turnip greens or kale. Look for it in larger grocery stores. Try it, too, in a Bloody Mary, stirred into soup or drizzled over huevos rancheros.

Grilled Artichokes with Smoked Aioli

MAKES: 6 servings • **PREP:** 40 minutes • **SOAK:** 20 minutes • **COOK:** 40 to 45 minutes

Don't be intimidated by artichokes. They're really simple to prep, and grilling seems to intensify their flavor. The smoked aioli can be served with any grilled vegetables or as a spread for sandwiches.

2 lemons, cut in half

6 artichokes

Kosher salt and finely ground black pepper to taste

Smoked Aioli

3 cloves Smoked Garlic (page 15)

¾ cup good-quality mayonnaise, such as Hellmann's or Duke's

2 tbsp freshly squeezed lemon juice

2 tsp Dijon mustard

1 tsp Worcestershire sauce

Lemon wedges and finely grated lemon zest for garnish

1. Squeeze 2 of the lemon halves into a large bowl of cold water. Trim the artichokes by cutting off the tough outer leaves with scissors. Cut the artichokes in half lengthwise and submerge them in the lemon water for 20 minutes, weighing the artichoke halves down with a small plate if they float. **2.** Drain the artichoke halves and pat dry. Using a melon baller, cut out the hairy choke from the center of each artichoke half. Use a potato peeler to trim the hard outer part of the stems. **3.** Prepare your grill for indirect cooking and preheat it to 250°F. Season the artichoke halves with salt and pepper to taste. Place, cut sides up, on the grill. **4.** Grill the artichoke halves until their hearts and stems are tender, 40 to 45 minutes. Remove the artichoke hearts from the grill, put in a large bowl and cover tightly with plastic wrap. Set aside. **5.** For the Smoked Aioli, squeeze the smoked garlic cloves from their skins into a food processor. Add the mayonnaise, lemon juice, mustard and Worcestershire sauce. Pulse until very smooth. **6.** Scrape the aioli into a fine-mesh sieve. Rub through the sieve into a small bowl. **7.** Arrange the artichoke halves on a serving platter. Drizzle with some of the aioli and sprinkle with lemon zest. Serve immediately with lemon wedges and the remaining aioli.

Q SAVVY

Add extra zip to the Smoked Aioli by stirring in 1 tsp minced canned chipotles in adobo sauce.

Smoked Beets with Goat Cheese

MAKES: 6 to 8 servings • **PREP:** 20 minutes • **COOK:** about 3 hours

One of my favorite restaurants in Austin, TX, is Freedmen's Bar. Chef Evan LeRoy serves up brilliant barbecue, including an amazing smoked beet dish, which was the inspiration for this recipe.

2 lb mixed golden and red beets, peeled and trimmed

½ cup water

¼ cup canola oil

2 tbsp red wine vinegar

1 bunch fresh thyme

Kosher salt and finely ground black pepper to taste

Sugar maple wood chips

1 cup crumbled goat cheese

1. Prepare your smoker or grill for direct cooking and preheat it to medium-high (375°F to 450°F). **2.** Grill the whole beets, turning often, until lightly charred, 4 to 6 minutes. **3.** Remove the beets from the grill and cut into quarters. Combine the beets, water, oil, vinegar, bunch of thyme, and salt and pepper to taste in a cast iron skillet. **4.** Prepare the smoker or grill for indirect cooking and reduce the temperature to 250°F. Add a handful of sugar maple chips, following the instructions on page 9 for your type of smoker or grill. **5.** When the chips start to smoke, place the skillet containing the beets on the cool side of the grill. Smoke until the beets are tender, turning them often and adding a little water, if necessary, to keep the beets hydrated and glossy, 2 to 3 hours. Replenish the wood chips by adding another handful every 30 minutes while the beets cook. **6.** Just before serving, sprinkle the beets with goat cheese.

Q SAVVY

To avoid staining your hands, wear gloves when cutting beets, and use a nonporous cutting board for easy cleanup.

Grilled Paneer and Charred Rapini
Photo on page 194

MAKES: 4 servings • **PREP:** 20 minutes • **COOK:** 8 to 12 minutes

Paneer, an Indian cow's milk cheese available in South Asian grocery stores, is great on the grill. Its mild flavor makes it a blank canvas ready to take on whatever seasonings you wish to add. Make sure your grill is super clean and lightly oiled before grilling paneer.

½ tsp ground coriander

½ tsp galangal powder (see sidebar)

½ tsp chili powder

½ tsp kosher salt

½ tsp finely ground black pepper

1 piece (14 oz) paneer, cut into ½-inch slices

1 bunch rapini, washed

2 tbsp extra virgin olive oil

¼ cup best-quality balsamic syrup

1. Mix together the coriander, galangal, chili powder, salt and pepper in a small bowl. Sprinkle the spice mixture over the paneer slices and set aside. **2.** Prepare your grill for direct cooking and preheat it to high (450°F-plus). Toss the rapini in the olive oil. Grill the rapini, turning often, until charred and tender, 4 to 6 minutes. Remove the rapini from the grill and set aside. **3.** Clean the grill and oil the grates generously. Grill the paneer, turning once, until charred and softened, 4 to 6 minutes. Remove the paneer from the grill. **4.** Chop the rapini into bite-size pieces and place on a serving platter. Top with the paneer and drizzle with balsamic syrup. Sprinkle with additional salt and pepper to taste.

Q SAVVY

Galangal is similar to fresh ginger in appearance and flavor, but is milder and has notes of lemon and cardamom. Look for it in South Asian grocery stores.

Grilled rapini is a terrific side dish on its own. Toss it with balsamic syrup as soon as it comes off the grill, then serve sprinkled with freshly grated Parmesan.

Grilled Tofu with Tamarind Glaze

MAKES: 4 servings • **PREP:** 20 minutes • **COOK:** 12 to 24 minutes

I like grilled tofu—a lot. It provides a blank canvas for flavor, and this sweet-and-sour tamarind glaze works especially well.

1 pkg (14 oz/350 g) extra-firm tofu
2 tbsp canola oil
Additional canola oil for oiling

Glaze
¼ cup warm water
2 tbsp tamarind paste
1 tsp ketchup
1 tsp Dijon mustard
1 tsp minced garlic
Kosher salt and finely ground black
    pepper to taste

Q SAVVY

Make sure your grill is super clean and well oiled before grilling tofu; it can stick really easily and you won't want to deal with the mess.

1. Cut the tofu into 4 even-size slices. Brush each slice with canola oil. **2.** Prepare your grill for direct cooking and preheat it to medium-high (375°F to 450°F). Generously oil the grill grates. **3.** Grill the tofu, turning once, until lightly charred, 10 to 20 minutes. **4.** Meanwhile, whisk together all the glaze ingredients in a small bowl until smooth. **5.** When the tofu is lightly charred, brush the slices on both sides with the glaze. Grill for 1 to 2 minutes per side. Serve warm.

Smokin' Good Sweet Potatoes with Bourbon Butter

MAKES: 4 servings • **PREP:** 20 minutes • **COOK:** 1½ to 2 hours

Sweet potatoes are jewels of happiness. I love them any way, but especially with bourbon and butter.

Pecan wood chips
4 medium sweet potatoes, scrubbed
2 tbsp extra virgin olive oil
1 tsp kosher salt
¼ cup sorghum syrup (see page 133)

Bourbon Butter
¼ cup unsalted butter, softened
1 oz bourbon

1. Prepare your smoker or grill for indirect cooking and preheat it to 250°F. Add a handful of pecan chips, following the instructions on page 9 for your type of smoker or grill. **2.** Pierce the sweet potatoes in several places with the tines of a fork. Brush the potatoes with oil and sprinkle with salt. **3.** When the wood chips are smoking, place the potatoes on the grill. Smoke until the sweet potatoes are tender enough that the tip of a knife slides in easily, 1½ to 2 hours. Replenish the wood chips by adding another handful every 45 minutes while the potatoes smoke. **4.** Meanwhile, for the Bourbon Butter, whip the butter in a small bowl until light and fluffy. Whip in the bourbon. **5.** Split the sweet potatoes open and spoon 1 tbsp of Bourbon Butter onto each one. Drizzle with sorghum syrup and serve immediately.

Smoked Spaghetti Squash

MAKES: 4 servings • **PREP:** 20 minutes • **COOK:** 1½ hours

This recipe is so versatile. I serve it as a side or as a base for grilled meat, or cold with grilled shrimp, or my kids love it with pasta sauce (minus the pecans and maple syrup).

Pecan wood chips
1 large spaghetti squash (4 to 5 lb)
2 tbsp canola oil
Kosher salt and finely ground black pepper to taste
1 cup water
½ cup toasted chopped pecans
¼ cup unsalted butter, softened
¼ cup amber maple syrup

1. Prepare your smoker or grill for indirect cooking and preheat it to 250°F. Add a handful of pecan chips, following the instructions on page 9 for your type of smoker or grill. **2.** Cut the squash in half lengthwise and scoop out the seeds. Brush the cut sides of the squash with oil and season with salt and pepper to taste. **3.** When the wood chips start to smoke, place the squash, cut sides up, on the cool side of the grill. Pour ½ cup of water into the cavity of each squash half. **4.** Smoke, without turning, until the squash is tender, about 1½ hours. Replenish the wood chips by adding another handful every 30 minutes while the squash smokes. **5.** Carefully remove the squash halves from the grill and drain off any remaining water. Using a fork, scrape the softened flesh of the squash into a large bowl. Add the pecans, butter and maple syrup and toss well.

Smoked Slashed Potatoes with Chipotle Aioli

MAKES: 6 servings • **PREP:** 30 minutes • **CHILL:** 1 hour • **COOK:** 1 hour, 20 minutes

The proper name for these slashed potatoes is "hasselback," but we've always called them fluted potatoes in my family. Either way, they look gorgeous done on the grill, and they take the smoke so well. I love pairing these with Chipotle Aioli, which adds even more smoky warmth.

6 medium russet potatoes, scrubbed

¼ cup extra virgin olive oil

Kosher salt and finely ground black pepper to taste

Hickory wood chips

Chipotle Aioli

4 cloves Smoked Garlic (page 15)

1 cup good-quality mayonnaise, such as Hellmann's or Duke's

2 tbsp minced canned chipotles in adobo sauce

1 tsp freshly squeezed lemon juice

Kosher salt and finely ground black pepper to taste

1. Using a sharp knife, make crosswise cuts in each potato, about ¼ inch apart and stopping about ¼ inch from the bottom of the potato. **2.** Place potatoes on a microwave-safe plate. Microwave, uncovered, on high until the potatoes are just beginning to soften, about 20 minutes. Drizzle the potatoes with olive oil and season with salt and pepper to taste. **3.** Place all aioli ingredients in a food processor. Pulse until well combined. Cover and refrigerate for at least 1 hour before serving. **4.** Prepare your smoker or grill for indirect cooking and preheat it to 275°F. Add a handful of hickory chips, following the instructions on page 9 for your type of smoker or grill. **5.** When the chips start to smoke, place the potatoes on the grill. Smoke until the potatoes are tender, about 1 hour. **6.** Remove the potatoes from the grill. Serve topped with Chipotle Aioli.

Q SAVVY

To ensure you don't slice all the way through the potatoes, lay the handle of a wooden spoon on either side of each potato as you slice.

Grilled Polenta with Mushrooms

MAKES: 4 servings • **PREP:** 20 minutes • **COOK:** 10 to 15 minutes

This is a really gorgeous side dish or—for your vegetarian friends—a complete meal. I love the look of grilled polenta layered on a bed of salsa with a beautiful tumble of mushrooms on top. Commercially prepared polenta (wrapped in a sausage-shaped package) makes this a snap to put together.

Canola oil for oiling

1 lb cremini mushrooms

4 metal skewers

1 pkg (18 oz/510 g) polenta

4 portobello mushroom caps

Canola oil cooking spray

1 tbsp Christo's Green Herbed Salt (page 30)

1 tsp finely ground black pepper

Fresh Tomato Salsa (page 140)

¼ cup extra virgin olive oil

Kosher salt to taste

1. Prepare your grill for direct cooking and preheat it to high (450°F-plus). Generously oil the grill grates. **2.** Thread the cremini mushrooms onto the skewers. Slice the polenta into ½-inch rounds. Spray the cremini mushrooms, polenta and portobello caps with cooking spray and season with herbed salt and black pepper. **3.** Grill both types of mushrooms and polenta, turning often, until the mushrooms have softened and both mushrooms and polenta are lightly charred, 10 to 15 minutes. **4.** Remove the mushrooms and polenta from the grill. Slice the portobello caps. **5.** Spread a layer of salsa on a serving platter. Top with the polenta. Slide the cremini mushrooms from the skewers, then pile the creminis and sliced portobellos on top of the polenta. Drizzle with olive oil and season with salt and pepper to taste. Serve warm or cold.

Summertime Sangria

2 cups fresh blackberries

2 very ripe peaches, pitted and sliced thinly

¼ cup granulated sugar

1 lemon, juiced

1 bottle (26 oz/750 mL) Riesling

2 oz triple sec

Crushed ice

1 small bunch fresh mint, leaves picked

MAKES: 4 to 6 servings • **PREP:** 15 minutes • **CHILL:** 4 hours

I love the versatility of sangria. You can take just about any fresh fruit—peaches, berries, apples, pears—and make it your own. For a lower-alcohol version, add a 64-ounce (1.9 L) bottle of sparkling lime soda just before serving.

1. Mix together half of the blackberries, the peaches, the sugar and the lemon juice in a large pitcher. Mash the mixture until the sugar has dissolved. **2.** Add the Riesling, triple sec and remaining blackberries. Chill for 4 hours. **3.** Pour into glasses over crushed ice and garnish with mint leaves.

Smoked Mushroom Risotto

MAKES: 6 servings • **PREP:** 20 minutes • **COOK:** about 2 hours

At the Jack Daniel's World Championship Invitational Barbecue a few years back, my teammate Jessie and I were selected to participate in the I Know Jack . . . About Grillin' contest. We were given a box of random ingredients and a limited time in which to prepare them. Our box contained arborio rice, among other things, so Jessie and I decided to make risotto. We were crazy to attempt such a labor-intensive recipe, but we did—and we won. It was a sweet victory and the inspiration for this dish.

Oak wood chips

2 lb mixed cremini and button mushrooms, cleaned

2 tbsp extra virgin olive oil

Half white sweet onion, finely chopped

1½ cups arborio rice

3 cloves Smoked Garlic (page 15), smashed

5 to 6 cups simmering mushroom or chicken stock

1 cup freshly grated Parmesan

3 tbsp unsalted butter

2 tbsp fresh thyme leaves

Kosher salt and finely ground black pepper to taste

1. Prepare your smoker or grill for indirect cooking and preheat it to 250°F. Add a handful of oak chips, following the instructions on page 9 for your type of smoker or grill. **2.** Place the mushrooms in a disposable aluminum pan. When the wood chips start to smoke, place the pan of mushrooms on the cool side of the grill. Smoke for 1 hour. Remove the pan from the grill and set aside. **3.** Heat the olive oil in a large saucepan over medium heat. Sauté the onion until softened but not browned. **4.** Add the rice and garlic, stirring to coat the rice with the onion mixture. **5.** Add 1 cup of the stock. Cook, stirring, until most of the stock has been absorbed. Keep adding the stock, 1 cup at a time, letting the rice absorb the stock before adding more, until the rice is just tender, 45 to 60 minutes (you may not need all of the stock). **6.** Stir in the smoked mushrooms, Parmesan, butter and thyme. Season with salt and pepper to taste.

Q SAVVY

I love this smoked risotto with Cajun-Butter-Injected Turkey Breast (page 169).

Big Party Mac and Cheese

MAKES: 40 to 48 servings • **PREP:** 30 minutes • **COOK:** about 35 minutes

We have a few big parties every year where, if I don't serve my mac and cheese, people complain. Loudly. For months. This recipe makes a huge batch of mac and cheese, but it's perfect for sharing and sending home with people after the party is over. (It's great hangover food.) Canned cheese sauce comes in a variety of blends; we buy ours from a big box chain.

1 can (106 oz/3.13 L) cheese sauce
8 cups whole milk
1 cup bacon fat
¾ cup dried chives
3 lb cavatappi pasta
4 to 5 cups shredded cheddar
2 cups panko bread crumbs
2 cups crumbled cooked bacon

1. Preheat the oven to 350°F. **2.** Mix together the cheese sauce, milk, bacon fat and chives in a very large pot. Bring the cheese sauce mixture to a simmer over medium-high heat, stirring occasionally. Reduce the heat to medium-low and keep the sauce warm while you cook the pasta. **3.** In a very large pot of boiling salted water, cook the pasta until almost al dente. Drain well. Add the pasta to the cheese sauce mixture. **4.** Divide the pasta mixture among six 12- × 10-inch disposable aluminum pans. Top with (in order) shredded cheese, bread crumbs and bacon. **5.** Bake until the cheese melts, 10 to 15 minutes. Serve warm.

Stone-Ground Cheesy Grits

MAKES: 4 servings • **PREP:** 15 minutes • **COOK:** 20 to 25 minutes

For years I never understood the attraction of grits. It wasn't until another contestant at a competition let me try a bowl of their homemade stone-ground grits that a lightbulb went on. The grits were all comforting cheesy, creamy goodness. So skip the instant grits and make this beautiful dish for a warm hug on a cold day.

3 cups water
½ tsp kosher salt
1 cup stone-ground grits, such as Old Mill
1 cup shredded cold-smoked cheddar (page 18)
2 tbsp unsalted butter

1. Bring the water to a boil in a medium saucepan. Add the salt. **2.** Stirring constantly, gradually add the grits. Cook over medium heat, stirring constantly, until thickened, 20 to 25 minutes. **3.** Add the cheddar and butter, stirring until the cheddar has melted. Serve immediately.

Q SAVVY

I love to top these cheesy grits with leftover pulled pork, shredded brisket or meat pulled from leftover pork ribs. You can change up the cheese, too. Try smoked provolone or friulano instead of cheddar.

The Ultimate Mac and Cheese

MAKES: 16 servings • **PREP:** 45 minutes • **COOK:** 35 to 40 minutes

When you call something the "ultimate," it had better be awesome. This mac and cheese is beyond decadent and worth every penny you'll spend on cheese. You can add pulled pork, shredded smoked brisket or even buttery chunks of lobster to make this even more insanely good.

½ cup all-purpose flour

½ cup unsalted butter, softened

3 cups skim milk

2 cups half-and-half cream

8 oz chopped bacon

1 small red onion, diced

2 tbsp dried chives

1 tbsp mustard powder

2 tsp sweet smoked paprika

1 tsp granulated garlic (see page 25)

1 tsp finely ground black pepper

6 cups shredded cold-smoked cheddar (page 18)

1 cup shredded ash-covered goat cheese, such as Le Cendrillon

1 lb cavatappi pasta, cooked and drained

Kosher salt to taste

Topping

1⅓ cups panko bread crumbs

¼ cup unsalted butter, melted

2 cups shredded cold-smoked cheddar (page 18)

1. Whisk together the flour and butter in a large pot over medium heat. Cook, stirring often, for 5 minutes. **2.** Whisk in the milk and cream until smooth. Cook, whisking constantly, until the sauce is bubbly and smooth, 10 to 15 minutes. Remove the pot from the heat and set aside. **3.** Fry the bacon in a small skillet over medium heat until crispy. With a slotted spoon, remove the bacon from the skillet and set aside. **4.** Add the onion to the bacon fat in the skillet and sauté until softened but not browned. **5.** Return the pot of sauce to medium heat. Add the onion and bacon fat to the sauce and whisk to combine. Whisk in the chives, mustard powder, paprika, garlic and pepper. **6.** Add the cheddar and goat cheese to the sauce, a handful at a time, whisking until smooth before adding more. **7.** Remove the pot from the heat. Stir in the pasta. Season with salt to taste. Divide the pasta mixture among two 13- × 9-inch pans. **8.** Preheat the oven to 350°F. **9.** For the topping, mix together the bread crumbs and melted butter. Sprinkle the bread-crumb mixture over each pan of pasta, dividing evenly. Sprinkle each pan with cheddar and the reserved bacon. **10.** Bake until bubbly and golden brown, 10 minutes.

Q SAVVY

Sometimes, when I have a party, I make this mac and cheese in individual dishes, then bake them on the cool side of the grill while I'm cooking something else.

Portobello-Cheddar Burgers with Guacamole

MAKES: 12 servings • **PREP:** 20 minutes • **COOK:** about 15 minutes

Veggie burgers aren't known for their big, bold flavors. But try this one, stuffed with portobellos—the "meat" of the mushroom world—plus guacamole and cold-smoked cheddar, and you may never go back to regular burgers again.

12 medium portobello mushroom
    caps, brushed clean
12 slices cold-smoked cheddar (page 18)
12 ciabatta buns, split
½ cup unsalted butter, melted
Killer Guacamole (page 48)

Vinaigrette
¾ cup extra virgin olive oil
¼ cup balsamic vinegar
2 tsp minced garlic
2 tbsp Worcestershire sauce
2 tsp Dijon mustard
2 tsp finely chopped fresh oregano
½ tsp kosher salt
½ tsp finely ground black pepper

Optional Toppings
12 slices pepper Jack
12 pieces roasted red pepper
Thinly sliced radishes
Curly leaf lettuce

1. Prepare your grill for direct cooking and preheat it to medium-high (375°F to 450°F). **2.** Whisk together all the vinaigrette ingredients in a medium bowl. Brush the vinaigrette over the gill sides of the mushroom caps. **3.** Grill the mushroom caps, turning once, until tender, 12 to 14 minutes. **4.** Top each of the mushroom caps with a slice of cheddar. Grill until the cheese has melted, 1 to 2 minutes. **5.** Meanwhile, brush the cut sides of the buns with melted butter. Grill the buns, cut sides down, until lightly toasted. **6.** Assemble the burgers, spreading each with guacamole and adding the optional toppings of your choice.

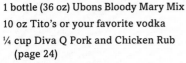

Ubon's Bloody Mary

1 bottle (36 oz) Ubons Bloody Mary Mix
10 oz Tito's or your favorite vodka
¼ cup Diva Q Pork and Chicken Rub
    (page 24)
Ice
5 drained pickled beans
5 stalks celery

MAKES: 5 servings • **PREP:** 10 minutes

This really rocks with the burgers. My favorite Bloody Mary mix is made by the owners of Ubon's Bar-B-Que in Yazoo City, MS (I've even used it straight from the bottle as a glaze for meatloaf), but you can substitute your preferred brand.

1. Mix together the Bloody Mary mix and vodka in a large pitcher. Add plenty of ice and stir. **2.** Rim glasses with Diva Q rub. **3.** Pour the drink into the glasses over ice, and garnish each with a pickled bean and a stalk of celery.

Grilled Vegetable Salad with Goat Cheese (page 229)

SALADS, SLAWS AND BREADS

What's a barbecue without a salad? These fresh-tasting sides, from both kitchen and grill, round out the perfect barbecue meal.

Grilled Caesar Salad

MAKES: 6 servings • **PREP:** 20 minutes • **COOK:** about 12 minutes

Who knew grilling lettuce could change a salad so much? Lightly charred leaves and a rich, garlicky dressing take Caesar salad from everyday to extraordinary.

3 romaine hearts
1 cup croutons
½ cup freshly grated Parmesan

Dressing
½ cup freshly grated Parmesan
2 tbsp freshly squeezed lemon juice
1 tbsp Dijon mustard
2 tsp anchovy paste
2 tsp minced garlic
½ tsp finely ground black pepper
2 tbsp good-quality mayonnaise, such as Hellmann's or Duke's
1 large egg yolk
¾ cup extra virgin olive oil
Kosher salt to taste

Q SAVVY

Make this a main-course Caesar by adding cooked double-smoked bacon to the salad or serving grilled shrimp on the side.

1. Prepare your grill for direct cooking and preheat it to medium-high (375°F to 450°F). **2.** Cut the romaine hearts lengthwise into quarters, leaving the root ends intact. Grill the romaine hearts, turning often, until lightly charred, about 12 minutes. Remove the romaine hearts from the grill and let cool slightly.

3. For the dressing, combine the Parmesan, lemon juice, mustard, anchovy paste, garlic and pepper in a food processor. Pulse until thoroughly mixed. Add the mayonnaise and egg yolk. Process until thick and creamy. With the motor running, add the oil in a thin stream. Process for 1 minute. Scrape the dressing out into a medium bowl and season with salt to taste and additional pepper, if necessary. **4.** Chop the romaine into bite-size pieces. Place the lettuce in a large salad bowl. Add the dressing and toss to coat well. Sprinkle with croutons and Parmesan. Serve immediately.

Cowboy Caviar

MAKES: 6 to 8 servings • **PREP:** 30 minutes • **COOK:** about 20 minutes

This salad travels well, so it's perfect for a picnic. Best of all, you can prepare it a couple of days in advance to let all the flavors come together. One of my favorite barbecue joints, Pork Barrel BBQ in Alexandria, VA, serves a great version of this. In a pinch, you can substitute thawed frozen corn if you don't have fresh corn.

4 ears corn, husked and silk removed

2 limes, cut in half

2 cups drained and rinsed canned black beans

4 roma tomatoes, seeded and chopped

Half sweet red pepper, seeded and minced

4 green onions, chopped

2 tbsp seeded and minced jalapeños

1 small bunch fresh cilantro, leaves picked and finely chopped

Kosher salt and finely ground black pepper to taste

Dressing

½ cup extra virgin olive oil

¼ cup apple cider vinegar

2 tbsp granulated sugar

2 tbsp honey mustard

1 tbsp minced garlic

1 tsp kosher salt

½ tsp finely ground black pepper

½ tsp chipotle powder

1. Bring a large pot of salted water to a boil. Add the corn and cook for 5 minutes. Drain well. **2.** Prepare your grill for direct cooking and preheat it to medium-high (375°F to 450°F). Grill the corn, turning often, until lightly charred, about 15 minutes. **3.** Add the limes to the grill, cut sides down. Grill until charred, 2 to 3 minutes. Remove the corn and limes from the grill and set aside. **4.** Whisk together all the dressing ingredients in a medium bowl. Set aside. **5.** When the corn is cool enough to handle, slice the kernels from the ears. Place the corn kernels in a large bowl. Squeeze the lime halves over the corn. **6.** Add the black beans, tomatoes, sweet pepper, green onions, jalapeños and cilantro to the corn. **7.** Whisk the dressing to combine. Pour over the vegetables and toss to coat. Season with salt and pepper to taste.

Q SAVVY

Cowboy Caviar goes really well with tri-tip steak or seafood. It's also a great healthy snack.

Grilled Panzanella Salad

MAKES: 6 servings • **PREP:** 30 minutes • **COOK:** 10 to 15 minutes

Grilled bread plus tomato, olive oil, pesto and cheese. It sounds really simple, but what you end up with is truly spectacular and bursting with flavor and freshness.

2 French loaves, each cut into six 1-inch slices

½ cup extra virgin olive oil

Kosher salt and finely ground black pepper to taste

2 lb cherry tomatoes

4 metal skewers

2 red onions, cut in half, leaving root ends intact

¼ cup freshly grated Parmesan

10 fresh basil leaves

Basil Pesto

1 bunch fresh basil, leaves picked

¾ cup extra virgin olive oil

½ cup pine nuts or slivered almonds

½ cup freshly grated Parmesan

2 cloves Smoked Garlic (page 15)

½ tsp kosher salt

½ tsp finely ground black pepper

1. Prepare your grill for direct cooking and preheat it to medium-high (375°F to 450°F). **2.** Brush the bread slices with olive oil and season with salt and pepper to taste. Thread the cherry tomatoes onto the skewers. **3.** Grill the bread slices and tomatoes, turning once, until lightly charred, 2 to 3 minutes for the bread slices, 4 to 6 minutes for the tomatoes. Remove the bread and tomatoes from the grill. Set aside. **4.** Grill the onions, turning often, until lightly charred, 6 to 7 minutes. Remove the onions from the grill. **5.** Cut the bread slices and onions into bite-size pieces and place in a large bowl. Remove the tomatoes from the skewers. Add to the bowl and mix gently. **6.** Place all of the pesto ingredients in a food processor. Pulse until smooth. **7.** Add the pesto to the bread mixture and toss well. Season the salad with salt and pepper to taste. Scatter with Parmesan and basil leaves.

Perfectly Pink Potato Salad Photo on page 47

MAKES: 10 servings • **PREP:** 20 minutes • **COOK:** 20 minutes • **CHILL:** overnight

Everyone has a favorite recipe for potato salad, and this is mine. My secret ingredient is sweet pimento paste, a Portuguese condiment that adds a hit of color and flavor. For best results, chill the salad in the fridge overnight before serving—it's worth the wait.

2½ lb mini potatoes

1 cup good-quality mayonnaise, such as Hellmann's or Duke's

½ cup sweet pimento paste

1 tbsp dried dill weed

1½ tsp celery seed

1 tsp kosher salt

1 tsp finely ground black pepper

½ tsp granulated onion (see page 25)

1 medium red onion, minced

¼ cup grated carrot

¼ cup finely diced celery

6 hard-cooked eggs, peeled and chopped (optional)

6 slices bacon, cooked and crumbled (optional)

2 tbsp finely chopped fresh chives

1. Boil or steam the potatoes just until fork tender. When cool enough to handle, cut each potato in half and set aside. **2.** Whisk together the mayonnaise, pimento paste, dill weed, celery seed, salt, pepper and granulated onion in a large bowl. Stir in the red onion, carrot and celery. **3.** Add the potatoes and the hard-cooked eggs and bacon (if using) to the mayonnaise mixture and toss gently. Refrigerate, covered, overnight. **4.** Just before serving, sprinkle the salad evenly with chives.

Q SAVVY

Food poisoning wrecks a party, so make sure to keep mayonnaise-based salads cool on a warm day. Set the salad bowl in a larger bowl filled with ice.

Grilled Potato and Chorizo Parsley Salad

MAKES: 4 servings • **PREP:** 20 minutes • **COOK:** 20 to 30 minutes

My friend Colleen would always bring a potato and chorizo salad to our potluck parties. It was so good, I'd try and put it out of reach at the back of the buffet table so there'd be leftovers. This is my grilled version of that salad that I'm now happy to share.

1½ lb mini potatoes, halved

2 tbsp extra virgin olive oil

Kosher salt and finely ground black pepper to taste

8 oz cured sweet Portuguese chorizo

1 small bunch fresh flat-leaf parsley, leaves picked and finely chopped

¾ cup crumbled queso fresco (see sidebar)

Vinaigrette

½ cup extra virgin olive oil

3 tbsp freshly squeezed lemon juice

1 tbsp Dijon mustard

Kosher salt and finely ground black pepper to taste

1. Whisk together all the vinaigrette ingredients in a small glass bowl, seasoning generously with salt and pepper. Set aside. **2.** Prepare your grill for direct cooking and preheat it to medium-high (375°F to 450°F). **3.** Meanwhile, put the potatoes in a microwave-safe bowl. Cover with plastic wrap and microwave on high until almost tender, about 8 minutes. **4.** Add the olive oil and a generous sprinkling of salt and pepper to the potatoes and toss well. **5.** Grill the potatoes and chorizo, turning often, until the potatoes are crisp on the outside and the chorizo is reheated, 10 to 20 minutes. **6.** Remove the potatoes and chorizo from the grill. Place the potatoes in a large bowl. Cut the chorizo into bite-size pieces and add to the bowl. **7.** Whisk the vinaigrette. Add to the potato mixture, along with the parsley, and toss well. Season with salt and pepper to taste and scatter with queso fresco.

Q SAVVY

Queso fresco is a soft, unripened cow's milk cheese from Mexico. Look for it in larger supermarkets or specialty cheese stores.

Shrimp, Mango and Noodle Salad

MAKES: 4 servings • **PREP:** 20 minutes • **COOK:** 10 to 15 minutes

Smoky sweet mango slices and spicy shrimp teamed with soba noodles make a satisfying salad that's super refreshing and perfect for school lunches. Out of mangos? Substitute a well-drained can of mandarin oranges and add directly to the salad without grilling.

1 pkg (9½ oz/270 g) soba noodles

1 lb medium shrimp, peeled and deveined

4 metal skewers

2 tbsp Moroccan Spice Rub (page 29)

Canola oil for oiling

2 mangos, peeled, pitted and cut lengthwise into ¼-inch slices

2 tbsp Piri Piri Hot Sauce (page 34)

1 English cucumber, thinly sliced

1 bunch green onions, finely chopped

¼ cup packed fresh flat-leaf parsley leaves

1 cup drained, shredded beets (from a jar)

Dressing

¾ cup rice wine vinegar

¼ cup granulated sugar

1 tsp toasted sesame oil

½ tsp table salt

1. Cook the soba noodles according to the instructions on the package until tender but not mushy. Drain well and set aside. **2.** Whisk together all the dressing ingredients in a small bowl until the sugar has dissolved. Set aside. **3.** Thread the shrimp onto the skewers. Season the shrimp with Moroccan rub. Set aside. **4.** Prepare the grill for direct cooking and preheat it to medium-high (375°F to 450°F). **5.** Generously oil the grill grates. Grill the mango slices, turning often, until lightly charred and just tender, 3 to 4 minutes. Remove from the grill and set aside. **6.** Grill the shrimp, turning once, until just opaque, 2 to 3 minutes. Remove from the grill and glaze with the hot sauce. Set aside. **7.** Toss the soba noodles with the dressing, cucumber, green onions and parsley. Spread the noodle mixture out on a platter. Top with mango slices, shrimp and beets. Serve chilled.

Strawberry-Rosemary Lemonade

2 sprigs fresh rosemary

¾ cup granulated sugar

3¾ cups water, divided

1 cup hulled, sliced strawberries

1 cup freshly squeezed lemon juice (about 6 lemons)

Lemon slices and additional rosemary sprigs for garnish

MAKES: 4 servings • **PREP:** 15 minutes • **COOK:** 2 minutes

This recipe comes from my friend Sara Lynn Cauchon, The Domestic Geek.

1. Put the rosemary sprigs in a small saucepan. Using a pestle or the back of a spoon, bruise the sprigs so they release their aroma. **2.** Add the sugar and ¾ cup of the water to the saucepan. Bring to a boil, stirring to dissolve the sugar. Remove the saucepan from the heat and let the syrup cool completely. Strain, discarding the rosemary. Refrigerate until chilled. **3.** Combine the strawberries and syrup in a blender. Purée until smooth. **4.** Stir together the remaining water, strawberry purée and lemon juice in a large pitcher. **5.** Pour into glasses over ice, and garnish with lemon slices and rosemary.

Grilled Vegetable Salad with Goat Cheese
Photo on page 218

MAKES: 12 to 14 servings • **PREP:** 30 minutes • **COOK:** about 15 minutes

There's nothing complicated about grilling vegetables, and I find that when I set out a large platter of this simple goat-cheese-topped salad, it always disappears fast.

4 small green zucchini, cut into
¼-inch slices

4 small yellow zucchini, cut into
¼-inch slices

4 small Japanese purple eggplants, cut in half lengthwise

4 bunches green onions, trimmed

2 sweet yellow peppers, cut in half and seeded

2 sweet red peppers, cut in half and seeded

½ cup extra virgin olive oil

Kosher salt and finely ground black pepper to taste

½ cup balsamic syrup

¾ cup crumbled goat cheese

1. Place all the vegetables in a large bowl. Add the olive oil and toss well. Season generously with salt and pepper and toss again. 2. Prepare your grill for direct cooking and preheat it to medium-high (375°F to 450°F). 3. Grill the vegetables, turning often, until just tender, 3 to 5 minutes for the zucchini and green onions, 10 to 15 minutes for the eggplants and peppers. 4. Remove the vegetables from the grill. Slice the eggplant and pepper halves. Arrange all the vegetables on a large platter, alternating the colors. 5. Drizzle balsamic syrup over the vegetables and sprinkle with goat cheese. Serve hot or at room temperature.

Q SAVVY

Buy the freshest, most colorful vegetables for the best impact and flavor. Any leftover grilled veggies are terrific on a pizza or flatbread or added to spaghetti sauce.

Grandma P's Sweet and Tangy Slaw

MAKES: 12 servings • **PREP:** 30 minutes • **COOK:** 10 minutes

Grandma P always had a garden. She grew onions, cabbages, potatoes, carrots and peas. A childhood memory is getting yelled at for eating all her peas and feeding spring onions to her dog, Brandy. Another memory is Grandma P's slaw. It was always in her fridge and it kept for weeks, becoming more intensely flavored each day. Tangy and sweet, it makes a simple summer side that's crunchy and delicious.

1 green cabbage (about 3 lb), cored and shredded

3 stalks celery, thinly sliced

2 carrots, grated

1 medium white onion, finely chopped

1 small red cabbage (about 1½ lb), cored and shredded

Dressing

¾ cup granulated sugar

½ cup canola oil

½ cup apple cider vinegar

2 tsp celery seed

Kosher salt and finely ground black pepper to taste

1. Mix together the green cabbage, celery, carrots and onion in a large bowl. **2.** Whisk together all the dressing ingredients in a small saucepan. Bring to a boil, then boil, stirring occasionally, for 10 minutes. Remove the saucepan from the heat and let cool slightly. **3.** Pour the dressing over the cabbage mixture. Refrigerate until chilled. **4.** Just before serving, add the red cabbage and toss well. Serve chilled.

Q SAVVY

Don't add the red cabbage until just before serving or your slaw will turn bright pink.

Creamy Carrot Slaw

MAKES: 6 to 8 servings • **PREP:** 20 minutes

Carrots are the star of this sweet, crunchy slaw. It's great for entertaining because it holds up well even if prepared the day before (just make sure to toss it a few times just before serving). It's a perfect pairing for pulled pork sandwiches, hot dogs, hamburgers or steaks.

½ cup good-quality mayonnaise, such as Hellmann's or Duke's

¼ cup extra virgin olive oil

2 tbsp apple cider vinegar

1 tbsp granulated sugar

1 tbsp honey Dijon mustard

1 tsp celery seed

1½ lb carrots, grated

3 cups shredded cabbage

Kosher salt and finely ground black pepper

1. Whisk together the mayonnaise, oil, vinegar, sugar, mustard and celery seed in a large bowl. **2.** Add the carrots and cabbage and toss well to coat with the dressing. Season with salt and pepper to taste.

Q SAVVY

Add some extra crunch to the slaw with slivered almonds or apple slices.

Three-Cheese
Smoked Garlic Monkey Bread

MAKES: 12 servings • **PREP:** 30 minutes • **COOK:** 35 to 45 minutes

This savory version of classic cinnamon monkey bread is ooey-gooey, garlicky greatness. I prefer to use a springform rather than a Bundt pan for this, as it's easier to remove the bread. This simple recipe is perfect for a last-minute get-together.

2 cans (each 4.5 oz/127 g) refrigerated biscuits (12 biscuits total)

¼ cup unsalted butter, melted

1½ cups shredded cold-smoked cheddar (page 18), divided

½ cup shredded mozzarella

¼ cup freshly grated Parmesan

12 cloves Smoked Garlic (page 15), finely chopped

¼ cup finely chopped fresh chives

Butter-flavor cooking spray

1. Open the cans and separate the biscuits. Cut each biscuit into quarters. **2.** Toss the biscuit pieces with the butter in a large bowl. Add 1 cup of the cheddar, the mozzarella, the Parmesan, the garlic and the chives. Toss well. **3.** Prepare your grill for indirect cooking and preheat it to 350°F. **4.** Generously spray a 9-inch springform baking pan with cooking spray. Scrunch a sheet of foil to form a 2-inch ball. Spray the ball with cooking spray, then place it in the center of the pan. **5.** Carefully spoon the cheese-covered biscuit pieces into the pan surrounding the foil ball. Top with the remaining cheddar. **6.** Place the pan on the cool side of the grill and bake, rotating the pan regularly, until the bread is golden brown and well risen, 35 to 45 minutes. **7.** Let the bread stand in the pan for 10 minutes before removing it. Serve warm.

Best-Ever Buttermilk Biscuits

MAKES: about 16 biscuits • **PREP:** 30 minutes • **CHILL:** 20 minutes (bowl), 5 minutes (biscuits) • **COOK:** about 15 minutes

To say I am a fan of biscuits would be an understatement. When you elevate the biscuit, the rest of the meal comes along for the ride. This is my Grandma P's recipe, but I'm also grateful to the many Southern ladies and gents who helped me get my biscuits to where I wanted them to be.

4¾ cups all-purpose flour, sifted

2 tsp good-quality baking powder, such as Clabber Girl

3 tsp good-quality kosher salt

1 tsp baking soda

8 oz unsalted butter (about 1 cup/ 2 sticks), frozen

2½ cups very cold, well-shaken buttermilk

¾ cup unsalted butter, melted

1. Chill a large stainless steel bowl in the freezer for 20 minutes before preparing the biscuits. **2.** Adjust the oven racks to the center and upper positions and preheat the oven to 425°F. **3.** Whisk together all the dry ingredients in the chilled bowl. Using the large holes of a box grater, grate the frozen butter into the bowl. Combine the ingredients with a pastry cutter until the texture is coarse and crumbly (do not use your hands for this). **4.** Add the buttermilk and, with a rubber spatula, mix just until the dry ingredients are damp (do not overmix the dough). **5.** Turn the dough out onto a lightly floured surface. Working as quickly as you can, pat the dough out into a rectangle and then fold it in on itself a couple of times. Handle the dough as little as possible; the more you handle it, the tougher your biscuits will be. **6.** Pat out the dough again into a ½-inch-thick rectangle. Cut into about 16 squares. (You can use a round biscuit cutter for this, but the trimmings make a much tougher biscuit.) **7.** Place 8 biscuits, ¼ inch apart, on each of two baking sheets lined with parchment paper. Chill the biscuits in the fridge for 5 minutes. **8.** Brush the tops of the biscuits with melted butter. Place the baking sheets in the oven, one on the center rack, one on the upper rack. Bake for 5 minutes, then swap the positions of the baking sheets. **9.** Bake for another 5 minutes, then swap the positions of the baking sheets again. **10.** Bake until the biscuits are lightly browned and risen, about 5 minutes more. It is important to not overbake the biscuits. **11.** Remove the biscuits from the baking sheets and let cool on a wire rack.

Q SAVVY

If you tend to have very warm hands, rinse them under cold water before patting out and shaping the biscuit dough.

Buttery Cornbread with Forty Creek Honey Butter

MAKES: 8 servings • **PREP:** 15 minutes • **COOK:** 18 to 23 minutes

Cornbread is a Southern staple. Do it right and it's magic; do it wrong and you've made a hockey puck. For the best cornbread you'll ever taste, use a well-seasoned cast iron skillet.

1 cup all-purpose flour

¾ cup cornmeal

2 tbsp granulated sugar

2½ tsp baking powder

¾ tsp table salt

½ tsp chili powder (optional)

2 tbsp unsalted butter or bacon fat

1 cup whole milk

1 cup shredded Monterey Jack

2 eggs, beaten

¼ cup unsalted butter, melted

2 jalapeños, seeded and minced (optional)

½ cup grilled corn kernels (see page 194)

Forty Creek Honey Butter

½ cup unsalted butter, softened

2 tbsp honey

1 to 2 tbsp Forty Creek Canadian whisky (to taste)

Q SAVVY

Day-old cornbread makes a great stuffing for a chicken.

1. Preheat the oven to 400°F. **2.** Whisk together the flour, cornmeal, sugar, baking powder, salt and chili powder (if using) in a medium bowl. Set aside. **3.** Add the 2 tbsp butter to a 10-inch cast iron skillet or a 9-inch round baking pan. Place the skillet in the oven until the butter melts, about 3 minutes. **4.** Meanwhile, whisk together the milk, cheese, eggs, melted butter and jalapeños in a medium bowl. **5.** Remove the skillet from the oven and swirl the butter to coat the bottom and sides of the skillet. **6.** Add the milk mixture all at once to the flour mixture. Add the corn kernels. Stir just until moistened (don't overmix). Pour the batter into the hot skillet. Bake until a toothpick inserted near the center comes out clean, 15 to 20 minutes. **7.** For Forty Creek Honey Butter, whip the butter until light and creamy. Fold in the honey and whisky until well combined. **8.** Cut the cornbread into wedges. Serve warm slathered with honey butter.

Blueberry-Lemon Cobbler (page 253)

SWEET SMOKE

Your barbecue adventure doesn't have to stop after the main course. There are lovely sweet endings here for your backyard bash. From the ultimate Death by Diva to a heartwarming fruit cobbler and a whole lot more, there are treats here to suit every taste and occasion.

Chocolate–Pig Candy Pretzels

MAKES: 12 servings • **PREP:** 30 minutes • **COOK:** 20 minutes

When I throw a party, I like to send my guests home with a gift bag containing some little nibble. This snack was born when I needed to fill fifty gift bags and had a large container of pretzel twists on hand. My kids loved helping me make these.

16 slices Pig Candy, finely chopped (page 110)

1 pkg (10 oz/284 g) honey pretzel twists

8 oz milk chocolate, melted

1. Spread the Pig Candy out on a plate. **2.** Dip one end of each pretzel twist in chocolate, then roll in Pig Candy to coat. **3.** Place the pretzel twists on a parchment-lined baking sheet until the chocolate has set. Store in an airtight container.

Hawg Chocolate

1 slice Pig Candy (page 110)

1 oz semisweet chocolate, melted

1½ cups whole milk

2 pkgs (each 1 oz/28 g) hot chocolate mix

1 oz bourbon

1 oz Frangelico

Whipped cream

MAKES: 1 serving • **PREP:** 10 minutes • **COOK:** 5 minutes

David Marks, of the barbecue team Wilbur's Revenge, serves up these warming mugs of spiked hot chocolate at competitions. At home, I like to team it with the Chocolate–Pig Candy Pretzels.

1. Dip the Pig Candy in melted chocolate. Place on a parchment-lined plate to set. **2.** Bring the milk to a simmer in a small saucepan. Whisk in the hot chocolate mix, bourbon and Frangelico. **3.** Pour the hot chocolate into a large mug. Top with a swirl of whipped cream and garnish with chocolate-dipped Pig Candy.

Chocolate-Pig Candy–Whisky Truffles

MAKES: 40 to 50 truffles • **PREP:** 1 hour • **COOK:** 5 minutes • **CHILL:** at least 5 hours

Bacon, chocolate and whisky are all high on my list of favorites. Combined in a truffle, they are wickedly indulgent. This is an adult-only dessert, but it's a showstopper.

20 oz best-quality semisweet chocolate, finely chopped

1 cup heavy (whipping) cream

2 oz Forty Creek or your favorite Canadian whisky

1 tsp vanilla

Topping

4 oz dark or milk chocolate, melted

8 to 12 slices Pig Candy, finely chopped (page 110)

1. Place the semisweet chocolate in a large heatproof bowl. **2.** Heat the cream to a simmer in a small saucepan. Pour the hot cream over the chocolate. Add the whisky and vanilla. Let the mixture stand for a couple of minutes. **3.** Using a rubber spatula, stir until the chocolate has melted and the mixture is smooth. Cover and refrigerate until firm, at least 4 hours or preferably overnight. **4.** Using a melon baller or a mini ice-cream scoop, portion out the truffles onto parchment-lined baking sheets. Refrigerate until firm, about 1 hour. **5.** Dip the truffles in the melted chocolate to coat them completely (I use a couple of fondue forks for this). **6.** Place the truffles on parchment-lined baking sheets. Top each truffle with pig candy. Chill before serving and store in the refrigerator or freezer.

Q SAVVY

Change up the flavor profile of these truffles by subbing rum for the whisky and other flavorings, such as orange or almond, for the vanilla.

Pig Candy Peanut Brittle

MAKES: 12 servings • **PREP:** 20 minutes • **COOK:** 10 to 12 minutes • **COOL:** 1 hour

Jennifer Hall, who gave me this peanut brittle recipe, is someone I met through Twitter. She lives by the motto "Live, love and dream food." I took Jennifer's recipe and added my own spin with finely chopped Pig Candy, because bacon does a brittle good.

1 cup granulated sugar

½ cup light corn syrup

1 cup smoked Virginia peanuts (see sidebar)

2 tbsp salted butter

2 tsp vanilla

¾ cup finely chopped Pig Candy (page 110)

1 tsp baking soda

1. Line a large baking sheet with parchment paper. Grease the paper. Set aside. **2.** Mix together the sugar and corn syrup in a large microwave-safe bowl. Microwave on high until bubbly, 4 to 5 minutes. **3.** Stir in the peanuts. Microwave on high until the peanuts are dark gold, 3 to 4 minutes. **4.** Stir in the butter and vanilla. Microwave on high for 2 minutes. **5.** Stir in the Pig Candy. Microwave on high for 1 minute. **6.** Stir in the baking soda until light, foamy and thoroughly mixed. **7.** Pour the mixture onto the prepared baking sheet and spread thinly. Let cool for 1 hour, then break into pieces.

Q SAVVY

Look for smoked Virginia peanuts in bulk-food stores or, if you prefer, substitute cashews, pecans or walnuts.

S'more Better Dip

MAKES: 6 to 8 servings • **PREP:** 20 minutes • **COOK:** about 45 minutes

Everyone loves toasting s'mores over a campfire. But for a big crowd, it's easier to make a tray of this s'more dip. You can dunk just about anything in the sweet treat, from fresh fruit, cake cubes and cookies to salty pretzel sticks. I love using Skor toffee bits in this recipe, but feel free to add anything—chopped nuts, crushed cookies—to make it uniquely your own.

2 cups milk chocolate chips

1½ cups heavy (whipping) cream

1 pkg (14½ oz/408 g) graham crackers

15 jumbo marshmallows, halved

½ cup Skor toffee bits

1. Mix together the chocolate chips and cream in a microwave-safe bowl. Cover with plastic wrap and microwave on high in 30-second increments, stirring after each one, until the chocolate chips are melted. Stir until smooth. 2. Prepare your grill for indirect cooking and preheat it to 300°F. 3. Arrange some of the crackers in a single layer in a 12- × 10-inch disposable aluminum pan to cover the base of the pan completely. Pour the chocolate mixture evenly over the crackers. Top with marshmallow halves. Sprinkle with Skor bits. 4. Place the pan on the cool side of the grill. Cook until bubbling, 35 to 45 minutes. 5. Serve immediately with the remaining graham crackers.

The S'more

1½ cups whole milk

2 pkgs (each 1 oz/28 g) hot chocolate mix

2 oz vanilla vodka

Hot fudge sauce and graham cracker crumbs for rimming

Mini marshmallows for garnish

MAKES: 1 serving • **PREP:** 10 minutes • **COOK:** 5 minutes

This warming drink, from award-winning pitmaster David Marks of Wilbur's Revenge, a barbecue team from Skippack, PA, is like a kick-ass dessert in a mug. It's a natural with the dip.

1. Bring the milk to a simmer in a small saucepan. Whisk in the hot chocolate mix and vodka. 2. Rim a large mug with hot fudge sauce, then with cracker crumbs. 3. Pour the hot chocolate into the mug and float mini marshmallows on the surface. Serve immediately.

Elvis Grilled

MAKES: 2 pizzas (12 slices) • **PREP:** 25 minutes • **REST:** 1½ hours • **COOK:** 10 to 15 minutes

Get all shook up with this Elvis-inspired dessert pizza, topped with the King's favorite combo of peanut butter, bacon and banana. I add chocolate to take it completely over the top. Take care when eating this—you don't want to drip on your blue suede shoes.

26 oz pizza dough, fresh or frozen and completely thawed (see page 55)

¼ cup cornmeal for dusting

¼ cup unsalted butter, melted

2 tbsp granulated sugar

Canola oil for oiling (optional)

1 cup crunchy peanut butter

1 cup semisweet chocolate chips

1 cup chopped cooked bacon

2 to 3 bananas, peeled and sliced

Icing sugar for garnish

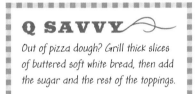

Q SAVVY

Out of pizza dough? Grill thick slices of buttered soft white bread, then add the sugar and the rest of the toppings.

1. One hour before grilling the pizzas, remove the dough from the refrigerator. **2.** Divide the dough in half and form into two 9-inch pizza crusts, crimping the edges of each as you would a pie. Prick the crusts all over with the tines of a fork. Let rest at room temperature for 30 minutes. **3.** Prepare your grill for direct cooking. Place a pizza stone (if you have one) on the grill grate and preheat the grill to 550°F. **4.** Dust a pizza peel with cornmeal and place the pizza crusts on it. Brush each crust with half of the melted butter and sprinkle with the granulated sugar. **5.** Dust the pizza stone with cornmeal or oil the grill grates. Slide the crusts onto the stone or grill grates. Grill until lightly browned, 3 to 5 minutes. **6.** Remove the pizza crusts from the grill and flip them onto the pizza peel so the grilled sides face up. **7.** Prepare the grill for indirect cooking. **8.** Spread each pizza with peanut butter. Sprinkle with chocolate chips and bacon. **9.** Slide the pizzas onto the cool side of the grill. Cook until the chocolate has melted, 5 to 10 minutes. **10.** Slide the pizza peel under the pizzas and remove them from the grill. **11.** Top the pizzas with the sliced bananas. Let cool for 2 to 3 minutes, then cut into slices and dust each slice with icing sugar.

Happy Hollow Hot Chocolate

1½ cups whole milk

2 pkgs (each 1 oz/28 g) hot chocolate mix

1 oz Jack Daniel's Whiskey

½ oz Kahlúa

½ oz Baileys

Whipped cream for garnish

MAKES: 1 serving • **PREP:** 10 minutes • **COOK:** 5 minutes

David Marks, of the barbecue team Wilbur's Revenge from Skippack, PA, brewed up this hot chocolate when I was trying to keep warm at the 2009 Jack Daniel's World Championship Invitational Barbecue. It certainly kept the cold out, and I'm sure the King would approve of serving it with his namesake pizza.

1. Bring the milk to a simmer in a small saucepan. Whisk in the hot chocolate mix, Jack Daniel's, Kahlúa and Baileys. **2.** Pour the hot chocolate into a large mug. Top with a swirl of whipped cream.

Death by Diva

MAKES: 12 servings • **PREP:** about 1 hour • **COOK:** 35 to 40 minutes

Death by Diva is my most requested recipe, but this is the first time I've shared it in its entirety. With this dessert I've garnered many perfect 180-point scores in competitions, often in contests where I've been competing against professional pastry chefs. Why is it so successful? It combines a little fruit, a little cheesecake, a little brownie and a whole lot of delicious.

36 strawberries (preferably organic)

2 pkgs (each 18 oz/510 g) Ghirardelli Double Chocolate Brownie Mix

1 (20 oz/600 g) plain New York–style cheesecake

2 cups semisweet chocolate chips, melted

¼ cup white chocolate chips, melted

3 cups whipping cream, whipped to stiff peaks

Raspberry syrup, such as Smucker's PlateScapers

Chocolate syrup, such as Smucker's PlateScapers

12 sprigs fresh mint

1. Using a melon baller, scoop out the stem end of each strawberry to make a hole. Place the strawberries, hollowed-out sides down, on paper towels to absorb their juices. Refrigerate the strawberries until needed. 2. Prepare your grill for indirect cooking and preheat it to 375°F. 3. Prepare the brownie mixes according to the package instructions, combining both batters in one bowl. Pour the batter into a parchment-lined 12- × 10-inch disposable aluminum pan. 4. Place the pan on the cool side of the grill. Bake until set, 35 to 40 minutes. Remove the pan from the grill and let the brownies cool completely in the pan. 5. Fill the cavity of each hollowed-out strawberry with cheesecake (do not use the crust). Reserve any leftover cheesecake. 6. Dip each strawberry into melted semisweet chocolate to half-coat them. Place the strawberries on a parchment-lined baking sheet. Chill until the chocolate is firm. 7. Drizzle the strawberries with melted white chocolate. Chill again until ready to serve. 8. Spoon the whipped cream into a piping bag fitted with a large tip. Set aside. 9. Pour a couple of tablespoons of raspberry syrup in the bottom of each of 12 martini glasses. 10. Crumble the remaining cheesecake (do not use the crust) and divide among the martini glasses, filling each half full. Top the cheesecake with a drizzle each of chocolate and raspberry syrup. 11. Crumble the brownies and divide among the glasses, filling them three-quarters full. Drizzle more chocolate and raspberry syrup over the brownies. 12. Top with another layer of crumbled brownies (you may have some brownies left over) and more chocolate and raspberry syrup. 13. Pipe whipped cream on top of each dessert. Garnish each with a cheesecake-filled strawberry and a sprig of mint. Serve the desserts with the remaining strawberries.

Grilled Angel

MAKES: 8 servings • **PREP:** 20 minutes • **COOK:** about 10 minutes

I have an obsession with grilling cake, and it's all because of Jacy and Rob Reinhardt of the amazing Prairie Smoke & Spice barbecue team in Saskatchewan. Jacy made grilled cake piled high with whipped cream and Saskatoon berries for a contest there, and I've been addicted ever since.

Chipotle-Chocolate Sauce

1½ cups heavy (whipping) cream
2 cups dark chocolate chips
1 tbsp unsalted butter
½ tsp chipotle powder
½ tsp vanilla

Cake

1 Bundt-shaped angel food cake (9 inches)
½ cup unsalted butter, melted
2 cups whipping cream, whipped to soft peaks
2 cups raspberries
Mint sprigs for garnish

1. Make the Chipotle-Chocolate Sauce by bringing the cream to a simmer in a small saucepan. **2.** Add the chocolate chips, butter, chipotle powder and vanilla. Stir until well combined. Remove the saucepan from the heat and set aside, stirring occasionally until the chocolate is melted and the sauce is smooth. **3.** Prepare your grill for direct cooking and preheat it to medium-high (375°F to 450°F). **4.** Using a large serrated knife, slice the angel food cake into 8 even-size pieces. Brush the cut sides of the cake slices with melted butter. **5.** Grill the cake slices, turning once, until golden and just crisp, 4 to 6 minutes. **6.** Place a slice of cake on each of 8 dessert plates. Drizzle with Chipotle-Chocolate Sauce. Top with whipped cream and raspberries. Garnish with mint. Serve immediately.

Uncle Rich and Kenny's Chocolate Cake Shots

4 lemons, thinly sliced
½ cup granulated sugar
1 bottle (26 oz/750 mL) Frangelico
1 bottle (26 oz/750 mL) vodka
Ice

MAKES: 32 servings • **PREP:** 15 minutes

When I was still a barbecue greenhorn, Rich Decker and Kenny Baker taught me a very important lesson. One evening at a competition, they brought over these shots that taste just like chocolate cake. I had a few too many and found out it's really difficult to focus on a barbecue competition with a hangover. Lesson learned. Stick to just a couple—and serve with the Grilled Angel—and you'll be fine.

1. Place the lemon slices in a resealable freezer bag. Pour in the sugar. Seal the bag and toss well. Set aside. **2.** Mix together the Frangelico and vodka in a large bowl. Add the ice and stir until chilled. Strain the mixture into a pitcher. **3.** Pour the drink into shot glasses and serve each shot with a sugared lemon slice. (Drinkers should suck the lemon slice before drinking the shot.)

Maple-Pumpkin Cheesecake

MAKES: 8 to 10 servings • **PREP:** 45 minutes • **COOK:** 1¼ hours • **CHILL:** at least 3 hours

Jennifer Carreiro Gardiner is one of the most talented bakers I know. Lucky for me, she is also one of my dearest friends. Jennifer has a knack for creating mind-blowing desserts, like this cheesecake. It's rich but not overwhelming, with a great maple flavor.

Crust

1½ cups ginger snap cookie crumbs (16 to 18 cookies)

¼ cup maple sugar or packed light brown sugar

¼ cup unsalted butter, melted

Butter-flavor cooking spray

Filling

3 pkgs (each 8 oz/250 g) cream cheese, softened

1 can (10 oz/300 mL) sweetened condensed milk

1 can (19 oz/540 mL) pumpkin purée

¼ cup maple syrup

1½ tsp cinnamon

1 tsp grated nutmeg

¾ tsp pumpkin pie spice

½ tsp table salt

3 large eggs, at room temperature

Topping

2 cups heavy (whipping) cream

¼ cup icing sugar

¼ cup salted pumpkin seeds

¼ cup maple syrup

6 slices Pig Candy, finely chopped (page 110; optional)

1. Prepare your grill for indirect cooking and preheat it to 325°F. Wrap the outside of the bottom and sides of an 8-inch springform pan in a double layer of foil. **2.** For the crust, mix together the ginger snap crumbs, maple sugar and butter in a medium bowl until crumbly. **3.** Spray the inside of the springform pan with cooking spray. Press the cookie mixture over the bottom of the pan. Set aside. **4.** For the filling, using an electric mixer, beat the cream cheese in a large bowl until fluffy. Gradually add the condensed milk and beat until smooth. **5.** Beat in the pumpkin, maple syrup, cinnamon, nutmeg, pumpkin pie spice and salt. **6.** Add the eggs, one at a time, mixing only until just blended. Pour the filling mixture into the springform pan. **7.** Bring a kettle of water to a boil. Place the springform pan in a large roasting pan. Place the roasting pan on the cool side of the grill. Pour boiling water into the roasting pan to come halfway up the sides of the springform pan. **8.** Bake until the edges of the cheesecake are set but a 3-inch circle in the center is still slightly jiggly, about 1 hour and 15 minutes. **9.** Remove the springform pan to a wire rack and let the cheesecake cool. Refrigerate for at least 3 hours or overnight. **10.** To serve, whip the cream until it holds soft peaks. Sprinkle in the sugar and continue to whip until stiff peaks form. **11.** Cut the cheesecake into slices. Top each slice with whipped cream, sprinkle with pumpkin seeds and drizzle with maple syrup. Sprinkle with Pig Candy (if using).

Award-Winning Cherry Dump Cake

MAKES: 8 servings • **PREP:** 15 minutes • **COOK:** 45 to 60 minutes

This recipe comes from Kim and Andy Groneman and their daughters, Lauren and Kaylin, who together make up the Smoke on Wheels Competition BBQ Team in Kansas City, KS. It's such a simple dessert, but it packs a big punch and has won numerous prizes for Lauren and Kaylin on the kids' barbecue circuit. Way to go, girls!

1 can (20 oz/567 mL) crushed pineapple, undrained

1 can (19 oz/540 mL) cherry pie filling

1 pkg (18 oz/517 g) yellow cake mix

½ cup unsalted butter, cut into small pieces

Raspberry sauce and whipped cream to serve

1. Prepare your grill for indirect cooking and preheat it to 375°F. **2.** Mix together the pineapple, with its juice, and cherry pie filling in a 10-cup round baking dish. **3.** Spread the dry cake mix evenly over the fruit mixture. Dot the butter evenly over the cake mix. **4.** Place the dish on the cool side of the grill. Cook until the top is golden brown, 45 to 60 minutes. **5.** Serve with raspberry sauce and whipped cream.

Very Berry Cordial

6 cups frozen mixed berries

4 cups water

2 cups granulated sugar

12 oz Tito's or your favorite vodka

½ cup fresh raspberries

½ cup fresh blueberries

1 lemon, zested into large strips

Crushed ice

MAKES: 6 servings • **PREP:** 15 minutes • **COOK:** 15 minutes

For an alcohol-free version, swap out the vodka for ginger ale or berry-flavored sparkling water.

1. Mix together the frozen berries, water and sugar in a large saucepan. Bring to a boil. Boil until the berries are completely softened, about 10 minutes. **2.** Strain the berry mixture through a fine-mesh sieve into a medium saucepan, pressing on the berries to extract as much juice as possible. Discard the cooked berries. **3.** Bring the juice to a boil, then let bubble, stirring occasionally, until it has reduced by half, about 5 minutes. Remove the saucepan from the heat and let the juice cool. Refrigerate until chilled. **4.** Stir together the reduced juice, vodka, fresh berries and lemon zest in a large pitcher. **5.** Pour into glasses over crushed ice.

Port-Smoked Pears and Crumble

MAKES: 6 servings • **PREP:** 30 minutes • **COOK:** 2¹/₄ hours

Here's an elegant dessert for a dinner party. The classic combo of port and pears takes on cherry smoke so well, and the ginger, star anise and cinnamon add pops of flavor.

3 cups ruby port

1 cup granulated sugar

2 cinnamon sticks

2 pieces (each 1 inch) candied ginger

1 whole star anise

3 firm but ripe pears

Cherry wood chips

Topping

1 cup packed light brown sugar

1 cup old-fashioned rolled oats

½ cup all-purpose flour

½ cup unsalted butter, cut into small pieces

½ tsp table salt

Q SAVVY

You can use any type of pears for this recipe, just adjust the cooking time slightly based on the size of the pears you choose.

1. Combine the port, sugar, cinnamon, ginger and star anise in a small saucepan. Bring to a boil over high heat. Reduce the heat and simmer for 15 minutes. Remove the saucepan from the heat. **2.** Meanwhile, peel the pears, leaving their stalks intact. Cut the pears in half lengthwise. **3.** Arrange the pears in a large cast iron skillet. Pour the port mixture over the pears. Set aside. **4.** Mix together all the topping ingredients in a small bowl. Set aside. **5.** Prepare your smoker or grill for indirect cooking and preheat it to 275°F. Add a handful of cherry chips, following the instructions on page 9 for your type of smoker or grill. **6.** When the chips start to smoke, place the skillet on the cool side of the grill. Smoke for 1½ hours, basting the pears every 15 minutes. **7.** Spread the topping over the pears. Smoke until the pears are tender and dark brown and the topping is golden brown, about 30 minutes.

Blueberry-Lemon Cobbler

Photo on page 236

MAKES: 8 to 10 servings • **PREP:** 30 minutes • **COOK:** 1¼ hours

Cobblers are heartwarming to me, and they're such a simple dessert to make. A bit of dough and some berries, peaches or other fruit. Let it bubble away 'til golden and sumptuous. That's it. Perfectly easy for anyone to do. Over the years I have had countless varieties of cobblers at picnics, backyard bashes and BBQ competitions. Play with different types of fruit—fresh or frozen—and make something you love.

Sugared Lemon Slices

2 lemons, sliced
¼ cup granulated sugar

Filling

6 cups fresh or frozen wild blueberries
¾ cup granulated sugar
1 lemon, zested and juiced
¼ cup water
3 tbsp cornstarch

Topping

¼ cup granulated sugar
1 tsp cinnamon
1 can (12 oz/340 g) Texas-style or regular refrigerated biscuits (10 biscuits)
2 tbsp whole milk

1. Prepare your grill for indirect cooking and preheat it to medium-high (375°F to 450°F). **2.** For the Sugared Lemon Slices, sprinkle the lemon slices with sugar. Place on the cool side of the grill. Cook until the lemon slices are dried out and caramelized on top, about 45 minutes. Remove the lemon slices from the grill and set aside. Leave the grill on. **3.** For the filling, mix together the blueberries, sugar and lemon zest and juice in a 9-inch cast iron skillet. **4.** Whisk together the water and cornstarch in a small bowl until smooth. Add the cornstarch mixture to the blueberry mixture and stir well. **5.** Place the skillet on the hot side of the grill. Watching closely and stirring often, cook until the mixture is bubbling and the juices have thickened, about 10 minutes. Move the skillet to the cool side of the grill. **6.** For the topping, mix together the sugar and cinnamon in a small bowl. Arrange the biscuits on top of the blueberry mixture. Brush the biscuits with milk. Sprinkle evenly with the cinnamon sugar. **7.** Bake on the cool side of the grill until the biscuits are thoroughly cooked and browned on top, about 20 minutes. **8.** Remove the skillet from the grill. Let stand for 15 minutes before serving. **9.** Garnish the cobbler with the Sugared Lemon Slices.

Q SAVVY

Canned peach slices also work well with this recipe. Drain them well before using and omit the sugar in the filling.

Apple and Salted Caramel Galette

MAKES: 8 servings • **PREP:** 30 minutes • **COOK:** 40 minutes

I hate making pie crusts, but free-form galettes, like this one, are easy and stress-free. Galettes are randomly shaped, and if one edge is a little thicker than the other, it's no big deal. I use apple pie filling for mine, but feel free to substitute cherry or blueberry if you prefer.

1 can (19 oz/540 mL) apple pie filling

½ tsp cinnamon

1 pkg (8 oz/250 g) cream cheese, softened

⅓ cup granulated sugar

2 eggs, divided

2 tbsp cornstarch

2 tbsp heavy (whipping) cream

½ tsp vanilla

1 refrigerated pie crust for a 9-inch pie

2 tsp all-purpose flour for dusting

½ cup caramel topping

½ tsp sea salt

2 tbsp water

2 tbsp turbinado sugar

Additional sea salt (optional)

1. Prepare your grill for indirect cooking. Place a pizza stone or baking sheet on the cool side of the grill and preheat the grill to high (450°F-plus). **2.** Toss the apple pie filling with the cinnamon in a medium bowl. Set aside. **3.** Using an electric mixer, beat the cream cheese and the sugar in a medium bowl until fluffy. Add 1 egg and the cornstarch, cream and vanilla. Beat until smooth. Set aside. **4.** Unroll the pie crust on a sheet of floured parchment paper. Using a spatula, spread the cream cheese mixture over the pie crust, leaving a 2-inch border around the edge. **5.** Stir together the caramel topping and sea salt in a small bowl. Drizzle half of the caramel mixture over the cream cheese layer. **6.** Top the caramel layer with the apple pie filling. Fold over the edge of the crust all around the pie. **7.** Whisk the remaining egg with the water to make an egg wash. Brush the edge of the pie with the egg wash. Sprinkle the edge with turbinado sugar. **8.** Using the parchment to lift the galette, place it on the pizza stone or baking sheet, leaving the galette on the parchment paper. Bake for 15 minutes. **9.** Rotate the galette. Bake for another 15 minutes. Rotate the galette again (rotating the galette ensures a nicely browned crust all round the edges). **10.** Bake until the apples are bubbling and the crust is nicely browned, about 10 minutes. Remove the galette from the grill and let it cool slightly. **11.** Drizzle with the remaining caramel mixture. Sprinkle with additional sea salt, if desired.

Drunken Pineapple Lollipops

MAKES: 8 servings • **PREP:** 15 minutes • **COOK:** 6 to 8 minutes

Arrr! There's something about the combo of rum and pineapple that always makes me want to talk like a pirate. Dress up these lollipops by serving them on a fancy plate with whipped cream and a sprinkling of toasted nuts, or keep things simple and just stack 'em in a pile.

16 peeled, cored fresh pineapple
   spears

16 metal or soaked bamboo skewers

½ cup salted butter, melted

¼ cup dark rum

1 cup dulce de leche or caramel sauce,
   warmed

1. Thread each pineapple spear lengthwise onto a skewer.

2. Mix together the butter and rum in a small bowl. Brush the pineapple lollipops with the butter mixture. **3.** Prepare your grill for direct cooking and preheat it to medium-high (375°F to 450°F).

4. Grill the lollipops, turning often, until lightly charred, 6 to 8 minutes. **5.** Serve warm drizzled with dulce de leche.

Q SAVVY

These lollipops are a great way to dress up vanilla ice cream.

Roadside Chicken (page 156)

WHAT YOU NEED TO GET YOUR GRILL ON

With the right grill and the correct tools, your
barbecue experience can be exceptional.
Here's the stuff I love to use.

CHOOSING YOUR GRILL

I don't believe there is one perfect grill—in fact, I own forty smokers and grills. While I don't suggest you invest in as many as I have, owning a variety of grills gives you different barbecue options. Here are some of my favorites:

I use the versatile **Big Green Egg** ceramic charcoal grill for everything from grilling to making pizzas. It's easy to use and maintains temperatures well (biggreenegg.com).

The **Char-Broil TRU-Infrared Commercial 4-Burner** grill is the only gas grill I own. I love the infrared technology, which results in fewer flare-ups than traditional gas grills (charbroil.com).

The insulated **Fast Eddy's by Cookshack Pellet Smoker Oven Model FEC100** provides consistent results, keeps food moist and is perfect for smoking large quantities of food. I use it for catering and competitions. Just set it and forget it (cookshack.com).

The **Ole Hickory Pits ACE BP** wood-burning barbecue pit is a convection-fan-system charcoal smoker that's easy to use and has a maximum temperature of 275°F (olehickorypits.com).

The **Onyx Oven** is an insulated cabinet, charcoal-fired water smoker. I like it because it's a convenient size and, since it weighs in at less than 100 pounds, I can tote it anywhere (bbqguru.com).

Stump's Smokers Gravity Feed Vertical Smoker Baby XL is an insulated smoker that's built tough (stumpssmokers.com).

Traeger Lil' Pig pellet grill offers the ease of a regular pellet grill in a cuter format (traegergrills.com).

Traeger Lil' Tex Pro pellet grill is excellent for making barbecue in the winter when you don't want to babysit the grill. It keeps food moist and is the easiest grill/smoker you'll ever own (traegergrills.com).

The **Weber Original Kettle Premium 22-inch** charcoal grill has been around forever. And for good reason. The grills last and are extremely versatile (weber.com).

The **Weber Performer Deluxe 22-inch** charcoal grill is an easy-to-light classic kettle grill with a built-in table (weber.com).

For the most versatile smoker right out of the box, it's hard to beat the **Weber Smoky Mountain Cooker 18-inch** charcoal grill. This one's great for learning fire control (weber.com).

THE GEAR YOU NEED

Having the right grilling gear makes barbecuing so much easier. These are the utensils I can't live without.

TEMPERATURE CONTROL

DigiQ DX2 from BBQ Guru uses power draft technology to make it easy to control the temperature of your fire (bbqguru.com).

The **Thermapen** thermometer is my number one grilling tool. It's accurate, it's easy to use and it comes in an array of colors (thermoworks.com).

ThermoWorks' **ChefAlarm** comes with a high-temperature cooking probe and features large digits and a backlight (thermoworks.com).

CUTTING BOARDS

Smoky Mountain Smokers' **disposable cutting boards** are handy for alfresco barbecues and their fold-up sides retain meat juices (smokymountainsmokers.com).

HAND TOOLS

 Silicone basting brushes are a hygienic choice, since they can be tossed in the dishwasher after using (grillpro.com).

 Big Green Egg's **Premium Three-Piece BBQ Tool Set** is a sturdy trio with rosewood handles (biggreenegg.com).

 I use GrillPro's **injection needles** exclusively. They're inexpensive and easy to use (grillpro.com).

 Char-Broil's **Premium Nylon Grill Brush** makes cleaning up a snap, and I love the ergonomically designed handle (charbroil.com).

BRIQUETTES AND OTHER FIRE STARTERS

 Nature's Own Sugar Maple Hardwood Lump Charcoal produces a sweeter-smelling smoke and higher temperatures than briquettes (basquescharcoal.com).

 Kingsford Competition Briquets are easy to measure so you get exactly the amount of charcoal you need (kingsford.com).

 The **Weber Rapidfire Chimney Starter** has outlasted every other one I have owned. It's a good design, but be cautious with the plastic handle (weber.com).

 Weber's **Lighter Cubes** are odorless, nontoxic and easy to light—even when wet (weber.com).

GRILLING SURFACES AND CONTAINERS

 GrillGrate grilling grates are great for obtaining perfect grill marks and speeding up any cooking process (grillgrate.com).

Frogmats smoking mats are handy when smoking small items that might otherwise slip through the grill grates (frogmats.com).

 Hands down, the best **pizza stone** I have ever used comes from Big Green Egg (biggreenegg.com).

 I love any utensil that serves several purposes. The GrillPro **Non-Stick Multi Roaster and Steamer** is one of my faves (grillpro.com).

 GrillPro's **Non-Stick Rib Rack** can be used to hold a roast, too, which makes it a must-have in my barbecue world (grillpro.com).

SKEWERS

 GrillPro's **metal skewers** heat up on the grill and help cook food more quickly (grillpro.com).

 GrillPro's 7-inch **bamboo appetizer skewers** are a handy size, and their flat shape makes them easy to turn (grillpro.com).

WOOD PLANKS

 Montana Grills' **Cross Cut Grilling Planks** offer superior flavor from the heartwood of a tree (montanagrills.com).

WOOD CHIPS AND SMOKER BOXES

 If you have access to a source of wood for **wood chips**, lucky you. I buy mine at Ontario Gas BBQ (bbqs.com) and big box retailers that carry GrillPro products.

 GrillPro's **Cast Iron Smoker Box** is easy to use and works with any type of grill (grillpro.com).

OTHER TOOLS I CAN'T LIVE WITHOUT

- Restaurant-grade **heavy-duty tongs**. I have lots, and keep one set for raw meat, another for cooked.
- Heavy-duty, nonporous USDA- and NSF-approved **cutting boards** from a restaurant supply store.
- Inexpensive, dollar-store **spray bottles**. I use them for spritzing and for flare-ups.
- **Bar cloths** for easy cleanup and removing grease quickly; these are essential to have on hand.
- Plastic, lidded **shakers** are perfect for storing and administering homemade rubs.
- A stainless steel **pizza peel** from a restaurant supply store lasts much longer than a wooden peel. As well as wrangling pizzas, you can use it for moving briskets, butts and large cuts of meat around on the grill.
- Stainless steel **mesh grill baskets** come in all shapes and sizes. I use these for grilling delicate foods like whole fish or small items that might slip through the grill grates.
- **Kitchen twine** is an excellent multi-purpose tool to have on hand for securing roasts and porchetta, or for tying basting herbs together.

RUBS, SAUCES AND INJECTIONS I LIKE TO BUY

I don't always make everything from scratch. These great-quality products are good to have on hand because sometimes you just don't have to reinvent the wheel.

Buster Rhino's rubs (bbqs.com)

Butcher BBQ rubs and injections (butcherbbq.com)

Caplansky's mustard (caplanskys.com)

Colins Creek Barbecue Pecan Rub (colinscreekbarbecue.com)

Granny's BBQ Sauce (grannyssauce.com)

Hav'n a BBQ sauces and rubs (havenabbq.com)

Hot Wachula's sauces and salsas (hotwachulas.com)

House of Q sauces (houseofq.com)

Plowboys Barbecue rubs (plowboysbbq.com)

Prairie Smoke and Spice BBQ sauces and rubs (prairiebbq.com)

Simply Marvelous rubs (bigpoppasmokers.com)

Smoke on Wheels marinade and injection (thebbqsuperstore.com)

Smoky Mountain Smokers sauces and rubs (smokymountainsmokers.com)

Swamp Boys sauces (swampboys.com)

Sweet Smoke Q Pork Juice injection (sweetsmokeq.com)

Texas Pepper Jelly and Craig's Sauce (texaspepperjelly.com)

Whiskey Bent BBQ Supply (whiskeybentbbq.net) is my go-to place for ordering all barbecue sauces and rubs

CONVERSION CHART

VOLUME		WEIGHT		TEMPERATURE	
¼ tsp	1 mL	1 oz	30 g	90°F	32°C
½ tsp	2 mL	4 oz	125 g	115°F	46°C
¾ tsp	4 mL	8 oz	250 g	120°F	49°C
1 tsp	5 mL	1 lb	500 g	125°F	52°C
2 tsp	10 mL	1¼ lb	625 g	130°F	54°C
1 tbsp	15 mL	1½ lb	750 g	135°F	57°C
4 tsp	20 mL	2 lb	1 kg	140°F	60°C
1½ tbsp	22 mL	2½ lb	1.2 kg	145°F	63°C
2 tbsp	30 mL	3 lb	1.5 kg	150°F	65°C
3 tbsp	45 mL	4 lb	1.8 kg	155°F	68°C
4 tbsp	60 mL	5 lb	2.2 kg	160°F	71°C
¼ cup	60 mL	6 lb	2.7 kg	165°F	74°C
⅓ cup	80 mL	7 lb	3.1 kg	170°F	77°C
½ cup	125 mL	8 lb	3.5 kg	175°F	80°C
¾ cup	185 mL	10 lb	4.5 kg	180°F	82°C
1 cup	250 mL	12 lb	5.5 kg	200°F	95°C
1¼ cups	310 mL			205°F	96°C
1⅓ cups	330 mL			225°F	105°C
1½ cups	375 mL			250°F	120°C
1¾ cups	435 mL			275°F	140°C
2 cups	500 mL			300°F	150°C
2½ cups	625 mL			350°F	180°C
3 cups	750 mL			375°F	190°C
3½ cups	875 mL			400°F	200°C
4 cups	1 L			425°F	220°C
1 pint (2 cups)	500 mL			450°F	230°C
1 quart	1 L			500°F	260°C
1 gallon	4 L			550°F	288°C
½ oz (fluid)	15 mL			600°F	315°C
1 oz (fluid)	30 mL				
8 oz (fluid)	250 mL				

LENGTH		PAN AND DISH SIZES	
¼ inch	6 mm	8-inch round pan	1.2 L
½ inch	1 cm	9-inch round pan	1.5 L
1 inch	2.5 cm	8-inch springform	2 L
1½ inches	4 cm	9- × 5-inch loaf pan	2 L
2 inches	5 cm	9-inch springform	2.5 L
3 inches	8 cm	12- × 10-inch pan	3 L
4 inches	10 cm	13- × 9-inch pan	3 L
5 inches	12 cm		
6 inches	15 cm		
7 inches	18 cm		
8 inches	20 cm		
9 inches	23 cm		
10 inches	25 cm		
14 inches	35 cm		

AND FINALLY...

THE GOOD LUCK SHOT

This has become a Diva Q tradition at every barbecue competition our team enters. We serve each of our friends a 1-ounce shot of chilled Forty Creek Canadian whisky (if there are children present, we pour them apple juice), then we recite the Diva Q Barbecue Competition Toast:

To family, to friends, to fire:
May your fires always burn clean,
May you always be surrounded by your true friends and barbecue family,
And may you all have the best damn barbecue cook of your life!

Then we bow our heads and recite together the Pitmaster's Prayer:

Our Pitmaster, Who art in heavenly smoke,
Hallowed be Thy bark;
Thy smoke ring come,
Thy meat be done,
on competition day as it is in barbecue heaven.
Give us this day our judging scores,
and forgive us for over or under cooking our meat,
as we forgive those who shigg* against us;
and lead us not into temptation,
to change our recipes on competition day. Amen

Written by The Blue Bloods, award-winning barbecue team

*Shigg: To enter a person's barbecue site with the intent of stealing barbecue secrets, in an effort to improve one's own barbecue score

From-Texas-with-Love Beef Ribs (page 131)

INDEX

Opposite: Diva Oysters (page 187)

ACKNOWLEDGMENTS

So many people have helped me, guided me and taught me invaluable life lessons. I could not have become who I am without my family and friends. It takes a village to help a person live their passion, and my village is awesome.

Vlad, I am and always will be the lucky one. Thank you from the bottom of my heart for believing in me. Thank you for your support. You are such an incredible man. I am blessed to have shared a part of your life. With much love. XXOO

Lexi, Ella and Gabe, you inspire me to live fully and show you that any obstacle can be overcome. You are my everything, and I love you to infinity. XXOO

Mike Miller, Patrick Weir and Jessie Sweeney, your support and encouragement have been no less than extraordinary. Many more adventures to come. XXOO

Paula Coulter and Rita Bishop, you are my extended family, my BFFs and all that. My home and heart belong to you both. Here's to our next adventure! I'll bring the whiskey. XXOO

My brother, Matt Bonawitz, I love you so much. Here's to us solving all of the world's problems. XXOO

Nick and Fanjia Dimovski and the rest of the Dimovski family—Mary, Johnny, Joseph and Nicholas—I am blessed to have had you all in my life. You are the most selfless people I have ever known. XXOO

Lisa and Harvey White, I could not have traveled anywhere without your help. Your support has been incredible, and I am indebted to you both for life. Love you so much. XXOO

Ted Reader, you're my big brother in barbecue. I can't even begin to thank you for helping me navigate my crazy life. Have I told you how great you are? Seriously, dude, you rock. XXOO

Jen and Jeff Gardiner, a girl could not ask for more in a friendship. You're a top-shelf duo. Thank you both from the bottom of my heart. XXOO

Billy Durney and Laurence La Pianta, you are two of the best sounding boards and voices of wisdom a girl could ever have. Thank you. Much love. XXOO

JoAnne and Tim, you never stop encouraging me. You always bring me up when I need it the most. No matter how many miles divide us, you inspire me always. Thank you for our never-ending friendship—it means the world to me. XXOO

My sisters-in-smoke, you know who you are and that you're some of the most BA women I know. I am inspired by your strengths and impressed by your resilience. You're among the toughest people on the planet and can grill like no others. XXOO

To my friends on bbq-brethren.com, you are some of the most outstanding people I have met anywhere. Ever. XXOO

The incomparable, absolutely kick-ass Ken Goodman, I am so honored you took the pictures for this book. It was a thrill to work with you. XXOO

Dave Raymond, you are the voice of wisdom I need. You are an extraordinary human being who makes the world a better place. XXOO

Gary Trotter and Brian Witteveen, you both believed in me right from the beginning. I am blessed and forever thankful for our friendship. XXOO

The awesome Robert McCullough of Appetite by Random House and Jennifer Bain, you both convinced me to do this book. Thank you for making me. XXOO

Many thanks also go to Basques Hardwood Charcoal, BBQ Guru, Butcher BBQ, Capital Appliance & BBQ, Char-Broil, Cookshack, Dickson Barbeque Centre, Granny's BBQ Sauce, Ole Hickory Pits, Ontario Gas BBQ, Smoke on Wheels Competition BBQ, Smoky Mountain Smokers, Stump's Smokers, Swamp Boys BBQ, Texas Pepper Jelly, TheBBQSuperStore.com, ThermoWorks, Traeger Canada, Traeger US and Whiskey Bent BBQ Supply.

Much, much love goes to my barbecue family. To be included in your company has been one of the greatest joys of my life. You are inspiring, engaging and thoughtful, and I am in awe of your kindness. There are so many to whom I am indebted. Thank you for believing in me. XXOO

Finally, thanks go to my fans. I am the luckiest woman in barbecue. I may not win most often, but I have the best fans on the planet. You are all awesome. Thank you for sharing your stories, emailing me, leaving great comments on my website and always asking for more. XXOO #unstoppable